Beating The Odds

64 Years of Diabetes Health

Table of Contents

Introduction

In early 2008 my friend, Lloyd, suggested that I should tell the members of our diabetes website about my early years with diabetes. I presented the idea to the membership and the response made it very clear that there would be much interest in the way a diabetic lived and survived in the 1940's and beyond. I wrote a series of blogs on my past experiences and included some of my autobiography. My story was very well received. I then posted the story on other diabetes websites. There were hundreds of replies saying that my story is inspirational and it provided hope for the futures of my readers. Some of my online friends suggested that I should publish the story.

I have now written this book to expand my story. My original story has been reconstructed and several new chapters, and pictures, have been added.

Some of the replies to my online story appear below. The many comments convinced me that my story should be published. I hope it serves to inspire diabetics to do everything possible to have good control of their diabetes.

"Thank you Richard for your story. You have given me hope. I was told in '84 that if I lived to be 30, I should consider myself lucky. You have proven that there is hope for us all."

"Richard, I finally found the time to catch up with the rest of your amazing story! It is a good read. You have chronicled the treatment of diabetes from it's infancy all the way through to todays technological advances from a personal point of view that I find fascinating! I am so glad that you refused to accept the Doctors' predictions as to your shortened life expectancy! I think your spirit of determination to beat the odds has had alot to do with your success at reaching a 'ripe old age' with none of the usual complications of diabetes."

"You take what you've learned and you pass it on and encourage and inform people and you do it all with such HEART and with complete unselfishness....Your attitude concerning diabetes and life in general is nothing short of awe-inspiring.... YOU ARE A+++++ in my book..."

"I have felt the happiness and warmth in your life. As well as some of the sorrow. Your chapters have touched each one of US in its own special way. Yes, I too believe that you have many more stories to come along and we will love them as much as we have enjoyed these chapters! I also want to thank you for your positive words of wisdom, and the strength that you bestow to others,,,,to endure living their life with D. And your kindness, in taking the time to answer all my questions!"

"Very interesting, very well written - cant wait for the next chapter.
I wish we could get this published."

"I think you are amazing!! And an inspiration to all diabetics! You inspire me to do and be better in my health choices. I have had diabetes for almost 40 yrs. and HAVE had some major complications,such as heart disease.,(heart bypass ten years ago in June) I,too ,have always struggled with change. I have turned down the pump,because of fear of changing things. You give me hope to make some major decisions and changes . I now am strongly considering going on the pump. Thank-you,Thank-you,Thank-you! Many more healthy,happy years are wished for you!"

"What a wonderful story! Thinking about that little boy with injections into the muscle with that huge needle brought tears of compassion to my eyes. The great thing about it is that you survived to tell the tale; to share your wisdom to help others. My 12 year old daughter was diagnosed with Type 1 diabetes only 7 weeks ago. I feel encouraged to read your success story so thank you so much for sharing it. I can't wait to read the rest! We live in New Zealand."

"Richard, I have read your life story here.... Very inspiring and uplifting, particularly to those caring for young children with Type 1.... it is reassuring to hear of the old timers who had no way to adequately measure blood sugar and were not even told about carb counting, yet there you still are, healthy and thriving.... I would really enjoy it if you went into even more detail and wrote a book. I might be able to find even more reasons why you have done as well as you have. We need to study you and those like you...."

"Ahhhh..... I didn't want the story to end. I just wanted to say I have enjoyed each and every chapter you have written. You are an amazing man with an attitude I admire so much! Thank you for all your help and advise you have given me! I appreciate it so much!"

****

The names of my family and my relatives are real. The names of my friends have been changed to protect their privacy.

Acknowledgments

To my Mother, Evelyn Cassell Vaughn,
and my precious wife, Anita Ellis Vaughn,
who gave me such tender,loving care.

To my sister, Shirley, for editing these pages.

To my friend, Barbra, for her computer help and
preparing this book for publication.

CHAPTER 1....My Early Years and Diagnosis

September 15, 1945 was the day. We had an appointment with a doctor in Salem, Virginia that day. He had ordered a blood sugar test to be done prior to that appointment. Mother and Daddy did not know what that test involved, or anything at all about "blood sugar". They had watched my health deteriorate over the preceding months and my pale, skinny body clearly showed I was very ill. There was much weight loss and no appetite. My other symptoms included drinking much water and passing urine frequently, in large amounts. I was weak and had very little energy for several months. My poor health began in early 1941.

I was born Richard Alvin Vaughn in Roanoke, Virginia on September 10, 1939. When I was two years old I had measles that settled in my ears. There was a fever that made me very sick. Mother told me I had three kinds of measles in nine months time. There was infantile measles, German measles (Rubella) and Red measles. Perhaps those illnesses lowered my resistance and began a spiral that led to more sickness in the years ahead.

In May of 1942 I had a hernia on my right side near my hip joint. It ruptured and I had to wear a truss. The rupture became worse and surgery was needed. There was such a long stay in the hospital that I had to learn to walk again.

My tonsils were removed later that year. There was some bleeding the first night after returning home and there were splotches of blood on my face the next morning. My parents thought that my throat had been bleeding. They took me to the doctor. He said rats had been biting me and had bitten through my lip. The rats had smelled the blood from the surgery. Mother's story did not say what was done to eliminate the rats. I do remember that big rat traps were set to catch rats while we lived in that house.

In early 1945, at five years of age, I had chicken pox and mumps, both within a few months time. Because of my previous illnesses and my hernia, I was already rather skinny and not very healthy. After partially recovering from the chickenpox and mumps I started losing weight and by mid-summer I was skin and bones. That was when all those symptoms began.

We saw a doctor but he had no diagnosis and he prescribed a tonic to help me regain my appetite. The tonic probably contained sugar and was most likely much the same as the old "snake oil" remedies that were not uncommon back then. The tonic was ineffective and we saw a second doctor. Still no diagnosis and it was the same with a third doctor. Mother and Daddy never gave up though and we saw a fourth doctor. He was the one who recognized my symptoms.

Despite my condition, my parents enrolled me in first grade at a nearby elementary school. There was a bathroom in one corner of the classroom. I spent much time there. Mrs Thompson, the teacher, became very annoyed with this despite the fact that Mother had explained my symptoms to her. Not long after school began that fall we were called and my parents were told that we should see the doctor the next day.

It is strange that I can remember where my family members stood in the doctor's office that day. Mother sat to my left and Daddy stood behind us with my two year old sister, Shirley, in his arms. It is easy to remember that day so clearly because there was a look on Mother's face that scared me when the doctor announced my "sugar diabetes". That expression on Mother's face is something I will never forget.

10

The doctor did not say a lot about my disease. He said that they should take me to the hospital and that there would be another doctor who would meet us there. We were told that doctor knew a lot about sugar diabetes and he would be my doctor in the years ahead. Mother was too frightened to say much. Daddy said nothing. Mother was always the one to ask questions in a situation like that, but this time, even she was almost speechless.

We met Dr. D. for the first time at the hospital. They gave me insulin and said that it would make me healthy again. The insulin was called beef and pork insulin because it was taken from cows and pigs. He told Mother and Daddy to never give me sugar, or any food containing a lot of sugar. Those were the only instructions Dr. D., the "diabetes expert", had for us. He was a far cry from an endocrinologist but we were told that he was the best doctor for diabetes patients in the Roanoke-Salem area at that time. Doctors knew so little about diabetes in the 1940s.

My stay in the hospital is all a blur, but the insulin did great things for me in a short time. My appetite was good and there was some weight gain. Insulin from pigs and cows saved my life and I regained much of my health. Insulin was discovered in 1921 and first sold in 1923. It was there for me only 22 years after it was first available.

So there we were with vials of insulin taken from animals, a glass syringe, and metal needles that were twisted onto the end of the syringe. The syringe and a needle were sterilized by boiling them on top of our stove every morning. Daddy gave one injection before breakfast each day. The insulin was a twenty four hour insulin.

We also tested my urine for sugar prior to my injection. A

blue liquid called Benedict's solution was poured into a large test tube, and 8 drops of urine were added. Then the tube was placed upright into a metal container and the water in the container was boiled. When the tube was removed the solution would progress in the colors of blue (with no sugar present), green, yellow, orange, red, and brick red or brown (with very high sugar present). A color change would indicate the presence of sugar. My urine was checked only once each day.

The needle was very long. It may have been about three quarters of an inch in length. We were instructed to stick the needle directly into the muscle on my arms or the top of my upper legs. The diameter of the needles was greater than the ones used now. That was necessary so that a piece of wire could be inserted to unclog them. The injections were very painful. I remember them very clearly.

My 6'th birthday was on September 10 that year and my diagnosis was on September 15. There was so much sickness from the symptoms of my diabetes. It was not a very happy birthday.

At six years of age I was too young to understand what was taking place. Candy and other sugar treats were not allowed and I am sure that disappointed me. There was really no other change in my rather normal life, except for the morning injections. Insulin made me healthy again and life went on as usual. I was a hapy and carefree kid. None of us knew how serious diabetes could be at that time.

I had also been a happy child before my diabetes symptoms began. There were blackouts in 1942 during World War II. On certain nights people had to turn out all their lights, in case of an attack. My old postage stamp collection contains some of the ration stamps my parents used during the war. After the war ended and the Allies were victorious, I went out in the backyard and ran about yelling that the war was over. The war having ended meant nothing to a five year old boy, but my parents were excited and some of their enthusiasm must have rubbed off on me. There are many things from my preschool years that are easy to remember.

Daddy and me, 1939

Mother had her appendix removed in late 1942. She was hospitalized for ten days. While she was there she learned she was pregnant. She also developed asthma and stayed very sick and nauseated until my sister, Shirley Ann Vaughn, was born on June 24, 1943.

Shirley was my first playmate and, as she grew older, we had good times together. We loved each other very much. Mother and Daddy did not have many friends. There were no other children in our neighborhood, so Shirley and I developed a very close relationship.

Pictures made before my diabetes symptoms.

Mother wrote her own story when she was in her 80's and she only briefly mentioned my diabetes diagnosis. She did not say anything about the months leading up to the diagnosis, or the trauma in the months that followed. My parents were devastated by my diabetes and not knowing how to care for me. The memories were probably too painful for Mother, and she chose not to include the details of that part of her life in her story. It is impossible for me to remember all of what happened back then, but my parents told me all the details years later.

My picture in first grade, age 6

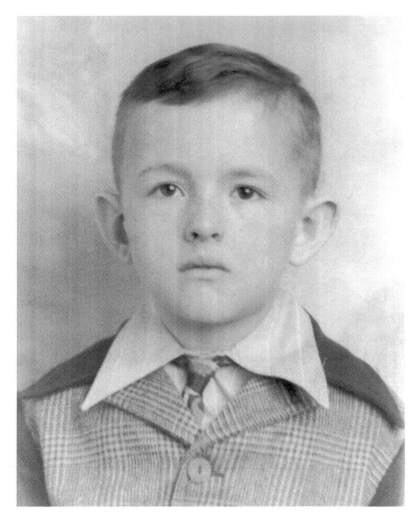

CHAPTER 2....First Years After Diagnosis

We did not know any other diabetics for many years during my childhood. It seems now that might have been a disease that diabetics would hide and be ashamed to reveal. I was a "closet diabetic" and never told any of my classmates in school. My teachers knew nothing about diabetes when Mother spoke to them at the beginning of each school year. None of my relatives had Type 1 diabetes, so far as we know.

There was one of my father's second cousins who was reputed to have some of the symptoms of Type 1 diabetes. She lost weight rapidly and died when she had stopped eating. There was never a diagnosis of her condition. Her parents may not have taken her to a doctor. Some of my relatives believed in home cures and medicines and did not go to doctors. Many mountain folks were that way back then.

My relatives did not talk to me about my diabetes. They talked to my parents in private. I will never forget one visit to my grandparents house one summer about a year after my diagnosis. While playing with my cousins, the door to the living room was closed. The talking in that room grew much quieter. My curiosity got the best of me and I pressed my ear to the door and listened. My grandparents, uncles and aunts were asking about me. That was the first time we had seen any of them since my diagnosis. It was a reunion of Mother's family.

They asked Mother if I was going to die. Mother had a hard time answering that question. She told them she did not know and that the doctor did not seem to know much about how she should take care of me. She explained that she never gave me candy, cookies and other food that contained a lot of sugar.

I felt guilty about eaves-dropping and went back to my cousins. Listening to the conversation was not a good idea, and I was very quiet on the way home. The thought of dying caused me to worry, but I don't recall it bothering me for very long . Death is a difficult thing for a young child to understand. Talking to my parents about it would have been a good idea. I will always remember that visit, like it was yesterday.

We went to visit one of Mother's uncles, not long after the family reunion. It was early one evening and my aunt wanted to serve refreshments. She took me by the hand and led me to a room down the hall. It was kind of dark in there, but there was enough light for me to eat part of the big Stayman Winesap apple she handed me. I wasn't really hungry. It was easy to hear the rattling of dishes where the rest of them were having cake and lemonade.

Their eating cake did not bother me. My feelings were hurt because my aunt did not want me to be with them. I never liked her after that visit. My aunt took me back to the living room after they were finished, but I just wanted to go home. There never was much of an explanation for what had happened. My aunt must have thought it would be cruel to have me see them eating cake.

Throughout my early years as a diabetic I had no major health problems and things went rather smoothly. I was always very skinny, maybe slightly underweight, until many years later. The urine tests showed high sugar almost every morning. There were, however, some nights that I had very bad hypoglycemic reactions. My bedroom was adjacent to my parent's room and the door separating the rooms was always left open. Mother was keyed in to my thrashing about and the moans she heard during my hypos.

She would jump out of bed and grab the glass of sugar water that was always handy. Daddy raised my body, and sat on the bed behind me, holding me while Mother slowly poured the sugar water into my mouth.

This usually worked very well, but there were times that my mouth was clinched so tightly that she could not get any of the liquid into my mouth. She would rub some of the liquid on my lips and I would lick my lips. This gave me just enough sugar and enabled me to relax. Then she could get me to swallow some of the sugar water. After coming out of those hypos I did not remember any part of what had happened. I was always so grateful that they took such good care of me at those times. There were many hypos until I was an adult, probably one per week on the average.

Mother had a very hard time with my diabetes, even though she was an excellent caretaker. She had terrible asthma during most of my preteen years. She smoked cigarettes that contained a kind of medicine. She would inhale the smoke and the medicinal vapor entered her lungs and helped her to breathe more freely. There was no tobacco involved. These cigarettes were prescribcd by our doctor. Mother would have a terrible time with her asthma after each of my hypos. She was a very nervous person and took medicine for her nerves.

Mother also had large varicose veins. They were causing her many problems and she wore elastic stockings to give herself some relief. A doctor suggested that she have the varicose veins removed from her legs. The surgery was very successful. She stopped wearing the elastic stockings and her asthma improved. After a few months she never again had asthma problems. Now how do you explain that? I was still having hypos and they still made her nervous, but there was no more asthma. Is it possible that the surgery had some connection? It does not seem likely, but we were all very happy that her days of terrible asthma were over.

At the time of my diagnosis we knew nothing of artificial
sweeteners. A few years later, a drug store was selling
saccharin. It had been used as an artificial sweetener since
1907, but we did not know about it until the late 1940's. It
was about that time that unsweetened Kool-Aid was
introduced. It was invented in 1927, and it made the scene
in Roanoke several years after my diagnosis. There were no
artificially sweetened drinks until we had the combination
of saccharin and Kool-Aid. The Kool-Aid was sold in little
bottles in concentrated liquid form. Kool-Aid was fantastic!

Mother used the saccharin and started making me pies,
cookies and other desserts. There was always one of her
delicious desserts for me for dinner and supper. There was
saccharin for cereal at breakfast and for lemonade in the
summer. Things were definitely looking up!! There were so
many carbs in the pies, cookies, and cereal, but we thought
they were OK, since they did not contain sugar. I ate
potatoes, corn, homemade bread and rolls, chicken and
dumplings (my favorite dish of all time) and the overload
of carbs caused me much high urine sugar. Oh how I wish
we had known back then that lots of carbs were very bad
for me.

There are many young diabetics who cheat and rebel after
being diagnosed with diabetes. Being diagnosed at the
tender age of 6, and respecting my parents, led to my never
questioning their demands involving my diabetes care.
Eating sugar or candy or other items containing sugar was
forbidden, unless my blood sugar was very low. I followed
that rule to the letter. Mother was so good to make me
wonderful desserts sweetened with saccharin. Their
desserts did not tempt me because those special desserts
she made were so wonderful.

Some of my favorite pies were banana cream, cherry vanilla custard, baked custard, chocolate, rhubarb, peach, and raisin. The pies had homemade crusts that were very thick, and they were divided into five pieces for my dinners and suppers. Can you tell I liked pies? There was also applesauce cake for my birthday and again for Christmas. The cake contained lots of nuts, raisins, and applesauce, to make it stay moist. Can you imagine how many carbs were in those desserts?

A typical breakfast had two kinds of meat, usually sausage cakes or thick country ham slices or bacon, which I ate with my eggs. There were homemade biscuits with lots of butter and I would dunk them in my saccharin sweetened homemade apple butter. That and a big glass of milk from our own cows completed my meal. It is not surprising that I had terribly high blood sugar....er....urine sugar, so much of the time. The breakfast was so large because both of my parents were raised on a farm and they and their families worked hard. They needed that food for energy when they set out to do their farming chores. My parents knew no other other way to live. We had three large meals every day and my daily carb intake was probably more than 500 grams.

When the peaches were ripe in our orchard I would climb up on the lower branches and reach up for a mellow, juicy peach. They were as big as a grown man's fist. After eating two peaches my tummy would hurt. With peach juice all over me I would go home to wash up. Daddy always sprayed our fruit, so all the fruit we ate was covered with dangerous chemicals. We did not know any better. It never hurt any of us so far as I know. We had plums, grapes, strawberries, raspberries, apples and pears. I ate too much fruit but it was so good!

Daddy put me in charge of the melon patch when I was

older. Planting cantaloupes and watermelons each year, and watching them grow, was a lot of fun. They required sandy soil and lots of water. They were left on the vine until they were fully ripe. The taste is so much better that way than when they are picked green and ripened afterwards. The same is true with all fruit and tomatoes. We provided our own meat, vegetables and fruit on our little farm. That was necessary because there was too little money available to buy all that we needed.

My parents did the best they could for me during my childhood. Dr. D. gave no instructions that helped. My parents raised me in much the same way they were raised in their mountain homes. They did not drink or smoke or swear. They were good Christians and kept to themselves. They bought land outside the city limits so that they could have a farm. They were raised on farms and loved that kind of living. That had a lot to do with the way I grew up and the development of my shyness and my overall personality. Telling you about my parent's background will help explain my life as a child, and help set the tone for my life as a diabetic while still living at home.

My family, 1945

CHAPTER 3....My Parent's History

My Mother's parents were John Henry Cassell and Penceannah Jane Cassell. They were born of small time farmers who owned their land. Their tools were plows pulled by horses, shovels, rakes and hoes. They were good, honest, hard working people. They lived in Portsmouth, Ohio, where their first three children were born. Their names were Verna, Eva and Dorothy.

When Verna was 18 months old she was diagnosed with spinal meningitis. She bore her illness with patience. Even in the face of death she had a smile for her parents. Verna died in 1910 and was buried in the family cemetery in Virginia, near where my grandparents were born. None of the other children ever saw Verna because she died when she was so young. Grandaddy was a flagman on the railroad and they moved to Roanoke, Virginia, while he had that job. My Mother, Evelyn Elsie Cassell, was born in Roanoke in 1918.

The family moved from Roanoke to Vesta, Virginia, shortly after Mother's birth. Grandaddy gave up his job with the railroad and bought several acres in the Blue Ridge Mountains near Vesta. He became a carpenter. In the next few years Leonard, James and John were born. My grandparents were very happy because their first four children were girls and they wanted some boys.

Many people were having diphtheria in the time my Mother was very young. Dorothy was diagnosed with diphtheria. In my Mother's story she tells of the doctor using some kind of pump and trying to pump the swelling out of Dorothy's neck. The doctor was a chiropractor and did not know how to treat Dorothy. Doctors were scarce in the area where they lived. Finally a medical doctor came and gave Dorothy shots of antitoxin, but he could not save her. She died shortly thereafter.

The family lived on a small farm in a region that was heavily wooded. There was only a dirt road for their wagon when Mother was very young. The entire family worked hard on their farm. Mother and two of her brothers hoed a very large field of corn every summer. They had to watch for snakes. They saw rattle snakes and copper heads rather frequently. Picking wild black berries was dangerous. Birds would eat the berries and snakes would lie there waiting to catch the birds. Mother was very careful to watch for snakes while she picked the berries. They say snakes are as afraid of us as we are of them. No member of her family was ever bitten by a snake.

Grandaddy became a skilled carpenter and he built his family a new home. It was a fine two story house with large rooms. There was a small brook and a spring a few hundred feet behind the house. About two miles downstream, where the forest was very dense, there were two men who had a still. They made moonshine. Grandaddy sent some of his kids to the still to get some of the mash to feed their hogs. The hogs loved it and they got very fat.

Frequently the ducks would wander downstream and eat some of the corn mash. The ducks were so full that their tummies would almost drag the ground. They waddled back to the farm, but they were very drunk. If they came home late Mother would go after them. She made a pocket with the front of her dress and ran through the woods picking up baby ducks. The family enjoyed watching the ducks come home. They would fall over and have a hard time getting up again. They were heavy with mash and drunk too. The family laughed at the spectacle.

When any member of the family got sick my Grandmother would use home remedies to treat them. The nearest doctor was very difficult to reach and a wagon and horses was their only means of transportation. My Mother's youngest brother was much younger than she was. Mother was in charge of him when he was a baby. She loved him like he was her baby, even though she was in her early teens. They formed a very close bond.

The first school that Mother and her sister and brothers attended was in sight of their house. It was a two room building with one room for school and another was the cloakroom. The winters were severe. They had to go through the fields and climb two fences to get to that school. There were not many students and only one teacher taught all the grades. School funds were low and there was a time that the school year was cut to four months. A grade could not be completed in four months, so the kids were running behind schedule.

There was no electricity in their home or at school. In school water was carried from a neighbor's spring in a wooden bucket and all the kids drank from a common dipper. Heat was provided by a wood stove and there were outdoor toilets. Mother attended that school through the fifth grade. At home they did their homework at night using a coal-oil lamp for light.

In 1925 Grandaddy bought a Chevrolet touring car. It had side curtains and a trunk mounted on the back bumper. He replaced the curtains with glass and that made the car warmer. He did not have any driving lessons and there were no driving permits back then. They were so proud of that car.

The schools in the area were consolidated in 1931 and Mother attended a school five miles from her home in Meadows of Dan, Virginia. She was placed in a room that had been a garage for sixth and seventh grades. There was still no electricity. Someone had taken a truck with a long bed and constructed a body of sorts with three long benches for seats. That was a makeshift school bus. If the bus made a sudden stop the kids all piled up in the front. After seventh grade Mother moved into the main building. It had four rooms. She finished her schooling there.

Mother was very intelligent and made very good grades. There were four seniors when she graduated. She was the valedictorian that year. Years later she liked to tell people she was the valedictorian in her high school graduation class, and then she added that there were only four seniors that year. Mother had a great sense of humor and that was one of her favorite stories.

We heard very little about Daddy's history. There is no story like the one Mother wrote and he talked very little about his past. If we asked him questions, he gave very short answers. He was a man of very few words.

My Daddy, Luther Bunyan Vaughan, was born in 1910, in a somewhat more populated community near Stuart, VA. His Mother was Nannie Lurinda Vaughan and his Father was George Abraham Vaughan. Daddy had a brother, Moir, and three sisters Bertha, Velda and Viola. There was also another brother who died when he was very young. The family lived in a small house on a farm. The owner of the farm hired my Grandpa to tend to the livestock and the crops.

When Daddy started school he spelled his last name Vaughn, but it was supposed to be Vaughan. His parents could neither read nor write and all of his siblings were preschool age. No one corrected his mistake. He was in high school before one of his sisters noticed. A few years later he had his last name legally changed to Vaughn.

Grandpa was unhealthy, and since Daddy was the oldest child, he took over most of the chores. He worked very hard on the farm. Later on Grandpa broke a leg and then was bitten by a copperhead snake. Daddy had to miss many days in school because he was needed on the farm. They did not want to be tossed out of the home they were using. Daddy failed that year and had to repeat one grade. He missed many days at school and was not well educated, but he was allowed to graduate. There was an understanding about children who were needed at home and allowances were made to accommodate them.

My Father tried to save his youngest brother's life by taking him on a horse and buggy trip to Stuart. This happened on a very cold day during the winter. His brother was very young. They wrapped him in blankets and laid him in the wagon. He had whooping cough and was very ill. He died before they could reach Stuart.

After graduating, Daddy found a job on the mountain near Mother's home. They met at the local store where he was employed. He was eight years older than her, but they dated and he met her family. The family liked Daddy very much. They were married in July, 1937. Mother was 19 and Daddy was 27. Mother was sick with tonsillitis on the day of the wedding. Grandmother did not attend the wedding. She thought Mother was too young, at nineteen, to get married. Mother asked her how old she was when she was married. Grandmother said "nineteen".

They had lived in their mountain homes far to the south of Roanoke, Virginia and life was very difficult there. They moved to Roanoke, hoping to find a better life. They settled in a very small cottage owned by Mother's uncle. The cottage was located in a nursery setting where there were hundreds of small shrubs and fruit trees for sale.

My Father took care of the nursery and sold the shrubs when people came to buy them. That was my Father's only employment at that time. I was born in that cottage on Sept. 10, 1939. A midwife saw to my birth there.

The Cottage In The Nursery

My parents answered the phone calls for the business and showed people the shrubs and fruit trees. Mother stated in her book for a particular day she sold four fruit trees for a dollar. That gives you an idea of how prices were back then. They got a 10% commission for all trees sold and they saved the money for Christmas.

A year or so after I was born the three of us moved to a rented house. It was a two story home with lots of big trees in the front yard. There was no plumbing in the house. There was a well and an old fashioned pump close to the back door. Water had to be carried from the pump to the house.

Daddy worked for awhile at the Roanoke City Mills. There was so much dust from the flour that he had to breath and he became asthmatic. He had to quit that job and he was unemployed. They were then drawing unemployment checks. He asked Mother if she was going to leave him. She told him no, and she would stay with him, even if they had to live in a hollow log. Stay with him she did, and they had a wonderful life and much happiness ahead of them.

Daddy & Mother, 1937

Much of what is in the first three chapters comes from my Mother's book that she wrote about her life in the year 2000, when she was 82. My Mother was a wonderful story teller. She made it very interesting. It would be wonderful if her whole story could be told here. It is on loose leaf pages typed by Shirley, my sister. Shirley gave me a copy of the story. I could not have written parts of these first three chapters without it.

Now to continue with my story and the years after my diagnosis.

CHAPTER 4....Our Farm

Before I was diabetic Daddy drove a milk truck and delivered milk to people's homes. The milk was in glass quart sized bottles and he had to carry several at a time while loading and unloading the truck. He developed hemorrhoids and had to quit that job. Then he was offered a job at the Roanoke Post Office. He began work there on June 24, 1943, the day Shirley was born. Mother was always a stay-at-home Mom and there was barely enough income to pay the rent on the house and put food on the table. The new job was a blessing. The salary was substantially larger than he had ever seen before. That was when they made a down payment on a ten acre property, not far from the house they had been renting. The land they bought cost them $700 per acre.

Grandaddy and my three uncles came and built us a four room house. He was a professional carpenter and he was training his sons to follow in his footsteps. The house went up very quickly. It had brick siding and no basement. There was just a crawlspace underneath and no insulation in the walls or attic. The only plumbing was one faucet in the kitchen. We had to walk about 100 feet from the back door to reach the outdoor toilet. That toilet was attached to the chicken house. Down the hill was a pig pen. Further along we had a pasture and there were two cows and a horse. We had a large orchard with many fruit trees and a 2.5 acre garden space. Yes folks, we had us a ten acre "farm". It was a lot of fun. I used to help stack hay. Shirley and I picked peas and beans and gathered fruit from the orchard. As we grew older we slopped the pigs and some days I milked the cows. A lot of good memories, but a hard life in so many ways.

A few years before we moved to our new location, we adopted a collie pup. She grew very fast. We named her

Pal. Mother told me she would jump up and put her front paws on me and knock me down. Animals were never allowed in our house. My parents felt that was unclean. Pal had to survive the harsh winters outdoors. She could crawl under the house to escape the ice and snow, but it was very cold and she suffered. She became very mean as she grew older and she chased the paperboy on his bicycle and bit him. The paperboy's mother brought him to our house the next day and showed us the boys wounds. They asked us to get rid of Pal. We gave her to Grandaddy's neighbors near their mountain home. Several years later we heard Pal had been bitten on the nose by a copperhead snake and she died. Here is a picture of Pal and me before we had our farm.

Every year we tended our crops and we provided much of our own food. Mother canned hundreds of quarts of vegetables and fruit. There were canned beans, tomatoes, tomato juice, peaches, applesauce, and much more. There was much more canning and I cannot remember it all. We had grape vines and there was canned grapes and grape juice. We made apple butter too. There were also cans of meat from our hogs that were butchered in the fall. Every year, when the hogs were killed and butchered, I thought about the fact that the insulin that kept me alive came from hogs. That did not keep me from enjoying the sausage, bacon, ham and pork roasts we had throughout the year. We had an old fashioned churn and we churned the milk and made buttermilk, butter and cottage cheese.

Eating was great! My Mother was an excellent cook!!! I ate carbs by the hundreds every day but avoided "sugar" and never cheated. We followed the doctor's instructions, but there was no advice about carbs. I had high urine sugar almost all the time. My blood sugar was tested at my doctor's office every six months. There were no other blood tests, that I can recall, until my teen years.

Daddy built a small barn all by himself and there were stalls for our cows and our horse. The doors were left open so the livestock could use the shelter during bad weather and at night. Two calves were born each year and, after they were fattened, we took them to the stockyard and sold them. The extra cash was much needed. My Father hitched the horse to a plow and plowed the 2.5 acre garden space every spring. It was very hard work for one horse, so Daddy tried renting a second horse. The rental was more than we could afford. A man offered him a mule, cheap. We soon found out why it was a low cost deal.

The horse and mule were both hitched to the plow. The mule refused to pull that plow. The horse would move and the mule just stood there. Daddy had worked on farms all his life and he approached the mule and spoke in soft tones. He fed the mule some corn. He took a special comb used to groom livestock and combed the mule on his sides and back. Then the mule was very cooperative and the plowing was done in no time. HEEEE HAWWWW!

There was one time, years later, that we did rent a horse. I approached the horse and tried to pet him. The horse reached down and grabbed a chunk of my abdomen with his teeth. After waving my arms and screaming, the horse let go and ran away. That horse could have caused me serious injury. I was lucky to have only a few heavy teeth marks and not much bleeding. I would rather have injections any day!! Another time Daddy had the horse hitched for some very light plowing. The horse keeled over in the middle of the garden and died. Daddy dug a very large pit beside the horse and rolled the horse into the pit.

We never had a horse after that. Later on that year Daddy bought a used tractor. We had a mowing machine and a hay rake that we hooked to the tractor. I drove the tractor and Daddy controlled the machines while riding them behind me. We mowed the fields and made hay for the livestock. We raked the hay and stacked it, making it ready for feeding the cows during the winter.

Daddy milked the cows at daybreak and cleaned their stalls. Then he ate breakfast and went back out and hoed or plowed the garden. He watered and pruned trees and shrubs and did so many other things. He would then go home for dinner and sleep on the floor for an hour afterwards. After napping he reported to the post office, where he worked from 2 PM until 11PM, with a one hour break for supper. The lunch pail Mother packed for him was unbelievable. He ate some of what we had at home for our supper.

Daddy would get home late and try to be in bed by midnight. I have never known a man to work so hard. On some days he made time to pick up a load of shrubbery at my uncles nursery and plant them at people's houses. We told people that Daddy had three jobs. The farm, the post office and the nursery. Daddy had a lot of muscle and was never much overweight. None of us were ever much overweight, even though we ate food like there was no tomorrow. I was always skinny until many years later, when I started using modern day insulins. We worked hard and we all loved each other so much. Good food, hard work and lots of love. That is my recipe for a successful family and growing up well.

The house across the street from ours was huge. It was made from big, beautiful stones like the ones in the buildings on the Va. Tech campus nearby. The people living in that mansion probably hated seeing us building a little four room house directly across the street from them. We were very surprised when they came over to see us. They welcomed us and were good neighbors. Their son Carl became my very best friend during my early school years.

We spent much time together playing cowboys and riding our stick horses, climbing trees, building a make-shift tree house, and hunting black birds that would land in our corn field with our BB rifles. They bought a TV set when they were first available at the stores. No one else we knew had one. It was so wonderful to get to sit in his beautiful living room and watch the black and white TV. That was so special! We were good buddies until we went to high school and then we drifted apart.

Shirley was four years younger than me. Carl, Shirley and I were playing Tarzan one day on our back property, no houses in site. There were about three acres of tall corn there. I was Tarzan, Shirley was Jane and Carl was Cheeta, the chimp. The corn field was our jungle. Carl and I were 8 and Shirley was 4. Cheeta and I went forth to hunt wild animals for food and left Jane in the middle of the jungle. We stayed away too long and we heard Jane crying. We were in no hurry to rescue Jane, so we took our time. When we got back to her, she was bawling. We led her out of the jungle and took her home. On our way we picked dew berries and ate them. I picked wild flowers for Jane...er...Shirley, and by the time we got home, she was happy and laughing.

Shirley and I still kid each other about that day. We tease each other and we have such a great sense of humor. Mother was nuts, so silly. We got our sense of humor from her. I don't remember ever doing any other cruel thing to Shirley. We love each other very much.

My parents never smoked cigarettes or drank alcoholic beverages. They were my guiding light and I intended to follow in their footsteps. When I was 10 a classmate named Bobby came to our neighborhood. He was in my homeroom, but was two years older than me. He had failed two years and was held back when I was in the fifth grade. He had never ridden a horse and wanted to ride our old work horse. So Bobby, Carl and I climbed aboard and we rode through the pasture. Bobby offered us cigarettes. Carl and I had never smoked, but we did not want to be called chicken, so we smoked a couple.

After Bobby went home we decided we would continue smoking after school each day. Carl took a pack of Lucky Strikes out of his father's pickup truck and we headed to his back property, where no one would see us. We smoked our way through several packs in a few weeks time. Carl's Father eventually caught on. He was missing his packs of cigarettes and his Mother had probably smelled the tobacco odor on Carl's clothes. One night after dark, Carl and his parents came to visit. That was most unusual and I knew something was up. Carl would not look at me and he hung his head. The jig was up. My parents were shocked to hear what I had done, but they did not discipline me at all. It was not necessary. Disappointing my wonderful parents like that made me feel so ashamed. They trusted me to never do anything like that again, and I didn't.

The smoking gave me very high urine sugar and caused me to have very little appetite. Things improved a lot in the weeks that followed. Except for abandoning my sister in the corn field, smoking was the only bad thing I can remember doing while I was a child.

The picture below shows Shirley, Carl and me riding our horse Maude. Our four room house is in the background.

My parents never used inappropriate language. Shirley and I were not supposed to use the word "sex". A funny thing happened when we were preschool age and Daddy was gathering turnips from the garden. He pulled an extra large one out of the ground and said "Boy that is a golly whopper!". Mother yelled at him to never talk like that in front of the kids. She was so disappointed in him. I had never heard her scold him in that way. Mother's actions made the incident very easy to remember. I rarely use a curse word now, even in anger. Only my wife and kids have heard me use a few very mild ones. Shirley and I always avoided curse words when we lived at home. My parents were good examples to follow and we were good followers.

Richard, Shirley and Carl (Tarzan, Jane and Cheeta)

CHAPTER 5....Elementary School And High School

My grades were not very good during my first few years of elementary school. My diabetes must have had a lot to do with that. All of my high blood sugar, and my parents not knowing how to deal with it, made school very difficult for me. There were a lot of C grades, but I never failed a grade. Mother was a great tutor and she helped me every day.

My hypos at night, and while playing hard during the day, caused Mother great concern. She was afraid I would have a hypo while at school and she would not be there to help me. She approached the teacher at the beginning of each year. She explained my diabetes and why there should not be any exercise for me during school hours. She convinced Dr. D. to write an excuse before school started each fall. So there was never any participation for me during play periods or gym. Sitting and watching the other kids at play was not any fun, but Mother had convinced me that hypos were likely if I was too active. Mother would not have it any other way.

My classmates knew I was different and they ignored me, but they never made fun of me. Making friends was very difficult for me because of my being so shy and withdrawn. Back then I blamed my diabetes for my not having friends, but in the years that followed, it became apparent that it was my shyness . My fear of having hypos while away from home made me appreciate Mother doing what she did. She always brought me out of my hypos at night, but there would be no one to do that for me at school. Sitting and watching the other kids play was OK. Knowing there would never be any hypos at school was very comforting. Having a hypo in school would have embarrassed me very much.

My grades began improving in the fourth grade. In the sixth and seventh grades there were several A 's and B's, not many C's. I was always the best in my class at spelling. When at home I was rather good at basketball. Daddy nailed a barrel hoop to the side of the corn crib and making baskets became easy for me. Mother watched over me when I exercised and did my farm chores.

Soon after starting eighth grade I had intestinal flu. I stayed at home several days and could not keep anything in my stomach. Under those circumstances my parents thought that they should not give me insulin. They were afraid my blood sugar would drop too low. They did not check this out with the doctor. After several days of no food, no water, no medicine, and no insulin, I could not lift my arms. I was barely able to move my head. The doctor came to our house and called an ambulance. My hospitalization lasted almost two weeks and my recovery enabled me to return to school.

Insulin users need to know that they need insulin even if they are not eating. They still need "basal" insulin under these conditions, but they do not need "bolus" insulin if they are not eating. The only insulin available during my school years was the beef and pork insulin. If my parents had known to give me some of that insulin during my illness I would probably have recovered without needing to be hospitalized.

The fear of having hypos while away from home was still present during my high school years, so there was no participation for me in gym classes. Participation during gym classes would have been very good for me in high school. I was mature enough to know how to take care of myself when my blood sugar was low. It would have been much better for me if I had rebelled and taken gym.

During tenth grade my home room teacher talked to my

classmates and praised me for making good grades. She used me as an example and encouraged them to make good grades like I did. That made me want to slink under my desk. I did not like being used as an example for my classmates.

My grades were the best in my home rooms, but I was not more intelligent than my classmates. They were active in sports and making friends and dating. I was reading my books and ignoring them. It was not until my senior year that I made a couple of friends. They were both males. Talking to girls was always scary for me, but I wanted to very much. Shyness and a lack of self confidence was characteristic of my parents and sister too.

My parents saved much of their money, and when I was in the ninth grade, they hired a contractor to build us a big, beautiful brick home. The four-room shanty was torn down. We were so proud of our new home! We had a color TV too!

I graduated number 13 in high school in June, 1957. During the graduation there were several scholarships announced. The valedictorian and salutatorian received scholarships for their academic achievements. There were several others given, but they were all athletic scholarships. That did not seem right to me. It made athletics seem more important than academics.

My senior year high school math teacher insisted that I go to college. She was my math teacher in my sophomore and senior years. My parents told me I could not do that. They thought I would not be successful because of my diabetes. They had no idea what college was all about, but they must have thought it would be very difficult, and too demanding for me. None of my relatives had ever gone to college. Many of them had good jobs and good salaries and they lived in fine homes.

My parents did not understand my being so obsessed with going to college. They did not understand that I was deeply hurt by their telling me that my diabetes would make college impossible for me. My goal was to show them and the world that college was not only possible, but that I could be a good student there! I had a good mind and I wanted to use it in a meaningful way. They begged me to apply for a job at the post office and become a post office clerk. Daddy worked there and he could keep an eye on me.

My choices were standing at a counter and selling stamps and weighing packages, or going to college. The only coed college available was Roanoke College, about 20 minutes from home. If there had not been a college nearby I would never have had a higher level of education.

My parents were disappointed in me and Mother cried. They were so dead set against my doing this that they refused to pay for any part of my tuition or my college expenses. They were kind though and agreed to give me free room and board. Daddy let me drive his older Chevy instead of trading it in when he bought a new car. He kept the car in good shape and paid for the gas. I had no money of my own, so a job with wages was very necessary. My uncle George worked at a local supermarket and he got me a job there. Work began the very month I graduated from high school. Working there 30 hours per week at 75 cents per hour enabled me to save enough money to pay for half of my tuition that fall. The other half of my tuition could be paid during the spring semester.

That summer was very rough. There was so much physical activity at the supermarket. Bagging groceries and stocking shelves made me very tired. My blood sugar ran low much of the time. Carrying the bags to the customer's cars was a regular activity for all of us "bag boys". Sometimes the customers wanted to carry their own groceries and I explained that the manager watched us bag boys. He would be disappointed if we did not do as he wished. There were signs on every grocery cart saying there was no tipping allowed. Many customers offered me tips, but I never took one.

It was as though the manager's eyes were on me and I certainly did not want to be fired for accepting tips. Actually, he was a very nice man and he would not have fired me, but that was not the way I felt about it back then. That extra walking and lifting was very difficult. Whenever there were few customers checking out we bag boys stocked shelves and changed prices on various items, as needed. A 30 minute break was allowed for each meal during my work hours. Testing my urine during my breaks was very important.

One very busy day my blood sugar was very low and I passed out and fell on the floor. My uncle George was there at the time and he knew what was wrong with me. After recovering, George told me that I ate the candy he had given me. That hypoglycemic episode wiped me out and I drove home after a long rest. George was sorry for me because he knew that my parents were not paying for my college expenses and my job was very important to me . He got me the job and watched over me like a parent. I will always be very grateful to him for everything he did for me.

As September approached I wondered if going to college was really a good idea. Working at the post office did not seem to be so bad after all. Common sense would always kick in and enable me to realize I had the brains for college and that was the right place for me. It was my goal to show all my doubters that I could be a good college student and my diabetes would not stand in my way.

My High School Senior Picture

I love country music

CHAPTER 6....My Undergraduate College Years

Roanoke College is affiliated with the Lutheran church and has always had a very good reputation. During the orientation before my freshman year we were told that college was going to be much harder than high school and we would have to spend much more time doing our homework. That scared me. With my job at the grocery store there might not be enough time to do all my studies and make good grades. It was also discouraging when some of the other incoming freshmen told me that they had followed the academic curriculum in high school. They had high school sciences like chemistry, biology and physics, and I did not.

The general curriculum was my chosen path in high school and going to college had never entered my mind until my math teacher in my senior year convinced me to do so. I was somewhat unprepared for college. Chemistry was a requirement during my freshman year for my chosen curriculum. There were no other students in the class who had not had chemistry in high school. There was no lower level chem course to prepare me like many colleges offer at the present time. It was very discouraging, but giving up and telling my parents I would not go to college would never do. That was not my nature. Doing my very best and failing would be better than never trying.

Architecture was my chosen field of study. There was a pre-engineering program at Roanoke College. The courses in my schedule would enable me to transfer after two years to Virginia Tech and become an architect. I made all A's and B's during my freshman year, except for chemistry. My lack of preparation for college chemistry was a big handicap. My chemistry teacher understood my problem but she could not do anything for me. My C's both semesters in chemistry seemed like a gift and I felt guilty about it.

Making new friends in college was easy and we visited each other's homes. We played golf and went bowling many times. They were good friends. I had a crush on several girls while in high school and during my freshman year of college, but my shyness kept me from asking them for dates. My first date ever was during my sophomore year of college.

One Saturday night it was my turn to stay after hours at the supermarket, to help with the mopping detail. Every aisle had to be clean and bright before we went home. Being so tired from the day's work made the mopping very difficult for me. On my way home that evening I thought my strange feelings were due to my fatigue, but while making a right hand turn at the first intersection, I collapsed at the wheel. The next thing I knew my parents were standing over me and a crowd of men were behind them. Several cops were there too. My wheels were not straightened during that right hand turn due to my hypo and my car went off the road and down a steep embankment into a creek bed.

My car had passed between two vertical posts that were supporting a huge bill board. Some people were measuring the distance between the posts and the width of my car, and they said the opening was about two inches more than the width of the car. My car had passed between the posts, but did not touch either one of them. I was not hurt and the car did not have a scratch on it. The guys standing in back were from a bar across the road. They had seen my car leave the road and they found my parent's phone number in my wallet.

Everyone but my parents thought I was drunk. There had never been any alcohol in my life at any time. My parents

50

told the cops about my diabetes. I don't think anyone there believed their explanation. There was no ticket though and a big wrecker pulled my car up the embankment later that night, or on Sunday. It was like the whole thing was just a bad dream. There were many hypos during my early years during my sleep or after a lot of exertion. There was no way for me to test my blood sugar before starting home that night.

Glucose monitors were not available until many years after that. My feelings and urine testing were my only clues to possible oncoming hypos. My parents thought that God had protected me and that was why I was not hurt. It was wonderful that my car was in good shape and I was able to attend classes Monday morning.

Not long after that incident Mother admitted that she and Dr. D. had been working together for my "benefit". When I was in elementary school Mother would phone him and tell him things that she wanted him to tell me before she drove me in for my appointments. I do not remember Dr. D's exact words but it went something like this: "Now Alvin, you can't drink or smoke. That will make your diabetes much worse." That was after my cigarette episode. "Now Alvin, you can't participate in gym at school, that will make your sugar go too low and you may have an insulin reaction." It is easy for me to remember Dr. D's voice and and mannerisms on those occasions. I always trusted him without question. It was very disappointing that Mother and the doctor were plotting and scheming.

Dr. D. also questioned my going to college but he did not sound as forceful as he had the other times. Mother admitted that she had called Dr. D. about college. Mother's attempts to control my life were out in the open, but we never argued about it. She knew I was disappointed in her and she said she was sorry. Daddy never knew anything about this.

My complete name is Richard Alvin Vaughn. While I was still an infant my parents decided they preferred my middle name. I was always called Alvin while growing up and in school. I now prefer being called Richard. I have always wanted to use my first name.

My attendance during my four years of undergraduate work was perfect. There were hypos while on campus, but there was never one that I could not handle myself. There were many lows that required my eating sugar from a small container in my pocket. There were no glucose tablets for a long time to come. Sugar worked very well. Some of my lows occurred during tests and my teachers never let me take a make-up test. They did not understand diabetes and hypos. Taking my tests with my class was required and there were no make ups given without a doctor's excuse. My worst low in college happened during a calculus test. It was so bad that my vision was blurred and reading my test paper was impossible. My teacher would not believe me. That was the only math test I failed in college. There were only three tests and a comprehensive final exam in each math course. My failing grade on that test resulted in a B grade for first semester calculus.

When arriving on campus for the first day of classes in my sophomore year, I was shocked to learn that the pre-engineering department had been discontinued. It was only an 80 minute drive to Virginia Tech, but we decided that would be too much for me. My income from the supermarket was necessary for paying my tuition. Driving home from Tech each day to work at the store would leave me too little time for my job and my studies. Continuing at Roanoke College was a must. My dream of becoming an architect was shattered, and it was tempting to quit college. Then Dr. Walpole, head of the math department, entered the picture. He knew my situation and suggested my becoming a math major. After hesitating for awhile, I realized that was better than quitting college. Being a math major was OK since it was actually my favorite subject in both high school and college.

Working 20 hours per week at the store and 30-40 hours per week during the summer, and whenever classes were not being held, was my work schedule for my first three years at Roanoke College. The manager at the store was very cooperative. With all those hours I was able to pay my way through four years of undergraduate school. The store manager even gave me days off when necessary, to give me more time to prepare for the harder tests and final exams.

Physics was required during my sophomore year. That was the hardest subject for me in undergraduate school. It was the same situation as with chemistry. Two more C's, but again I made all A's and B's for the rest of my grades that year.

Shirley had a friend named Linda. They went to high school together. I called Linda and made a date with her. It was my very first date. Weakness and fear overtook me while approaching her front door. It was too late to turn around and go home. There were two faces at the window looking out, with the curtain pulled back. She did not seem shy like me. She was sweet, pretty and had a great smile. My shyness made it difficult for me to talk to her. We went to a movie. That was a relief since I did not have to talk to her. I did not hold her hand. I felt like a miserable failure, but I asked her for a second date. She said yes!!! I probably just sat there in the car with my mouth hanging open, in disbelief. We continued dating, on and off, for four more years after that, but it was only a friendship. There were no dates with other girls until after my first year in graduate school.

A very strange thing happened during my junior year in college. A man from Paris taught my second year French class. There was a teacher exchange program and one of Roanoke College's English teachers went to Paris to teach and a French teacher taught for two years at our college. He was an excellent teacher. I loved the French language and he praised me for having excellent pronunciation of the French words. After giving an oral report on a French novel, he singled me out and told the class that they should all give a report like mine. That was very embarrassing and the situation made me feel very uncomfortable. There were friends of mine in the class who were giving me funny looks, but they never talked to me about it.

During the second semester there was a French play to be held in the college auditorium and my teacher wanted me to be the leading male character in the play. It took all the courage I had in me to give that book report. My appearing in the play was out of the question. He seemed to understand, but he was obviously disappointed.

I was concerned that my grade for the second semester would be affected by my refusing to appear in the play. I received an A and was relieved. He was going to return to France at the end of that semester. He approached me and asked me to consider going with him. He said my French vocabulary and my pronunciation were so good that I would fit in immediately. MOI??? I told him my intention was to teach math at the college level. Teaching had crossed my mind, but I was just trying to get out of this situation. He suggested my teaching math at a college in France. He wanted me to live in his home with him until a more suitable place was found.

He eventually seemed convinced that it was impossible for me to live and teach in France. He was disappointed but we were on good terms the last time I saw him. Should I have gone??? It is a good thing I did not go to France. There was a very wonderful life ahead of me here in the country I loved so much.

My junior year was my last year working at the store. I had saved enough to pay for all the tuition for my senior year. My grades had not been as good as I had hoped during my first three years of college because my job required so much of my time. I went to classes with incomplete homework. Falling asleep while studying at night after work hours was not uncommon. Fatigue was very commonplace with me, even when I had not worked at the store. At least some of that was probably due to my diabetes. Concentrating in class and on tests was difficult.

My grades would have been better if I did not have to pay my own tuition and work at that store. My senior year was different and I did not have to work at the store ever again. I made good grades that year and pulled up my overall grade point average. I graduated with honors. My parents and some relatives attended my graduation. I wanted to tell my parents, "See! You said I could not do this because of my diabetes, but I DID!!!" I never told them that. I'm happy that I kept my mouth shut. Working my way through college was good experience and it really helped me mature. I loved my parents and they loved me. Nothing ever came between us.

Shirley's and my graduations, June, 1961

CHAPTER 7....Graduate School And My First Love

Getting into a graduate level program seemed impossible. It was not affordable since I had no money left after graduating from Roanoke College. Getting a scholarship was beyond my wildest dreams. Dr. Walpole knew I wanted to attend Va. Tech and do graduate work in statistics. He wrote a letter to the Statistics Dept. at Virginia Tech on my behalf. They offered me a Fellowship. Unbelievable! The National Institutes of Health was the sponsor of the Fellowship. Va. Tech, at that time, was one of the top four schools in the country for graduate level statistics. There was much demand for statisticians nationwide.

Dr. Walpole had been my teacher for several courses during my undergraduate years and he thought I was a good candidate for the Fellowship. I did not think my grades had been good enough to get that kind of recognition. He must have written a glowing letter of recommendation. He knew that my diabetes had held me back and that I had to work my way through college during my undergraduate years. He may have included some of that background in the letter. The Fellowship paid all my expenses including room and board and there was some left over. I was in awe of the other beginning graduate students in my classes. Many of them had come from big name schools like Dartmouth and Stanford and some were from foreign countries. My background was insignificant compared to theirs. All of this made me feel very insecure and out of place.

Now let's get one thing straight! I am not super intelligent. I made good grades in high school and undergraduate college, but I had to study long and hard to get those grades. Some of my classmates studied much less and still made better grades. My intelligence is better than average, but I am nothing special. The other beginning graduate students talked circles around me, so how could I possibly compete? A "B" average was required in order to remain in graduate school and keep my fellowship. Keeping that kind of average in grad school was not going to be easy. The idea of working in study groups depressed me. The other members of the group would see how poorly prepared I was for graduate work. I had to hoof it on my own. It was by far the hardest year I had faced in college. A high "B" student from little Roanoke College did not have the preparation that "A" students from big name colleges did. There was no comparison.

I hated that year in grad school but managed to squeak through with a "B" average. The posted grades showed most of the other members of my classes had "A" averages for that year. Doubt and despair were with me again. Should I attend the second year? It would be a shame to throw five years of college away and not get the better job that an MS degree would offer me.

Standing before a group and communicating had always been very difficult for me. Something had to be done about that. I went back to Roanoke College one weekend that spring and talked to Dr. Walpole about a summer school teaching position. Someone had already been hired, but that individual learned that he had cancer just two weeks before my visit that day. He would not be available to teach that summer. Dr. Walpole was delighted that I wanted to teach. My mouth dropped and I wanted to run to my old Chevy and drive away. Was this actually happening? What was I getting myself into? HELPPPP!

I agreed to take the position. He wanted me to teach four classes that summer. That is unheard of in this day and time. A max of two classes is allowed at colleges for summer school now. Teaching four summer classes is like teaching eight classes in a regular semester. Elementary Algebra, Finite Math, Calculus I and Calculus II were the courses I taught that summer. Approaching my first class in June was frightening. My knees were so weak and I sat down fast so I would not fall down. Calling the roll gave me some relief. It was amazing that I got through that day. Things were going well by the end of the week. Incredible!

Testing my urine sugar with a product called Tes-Tape was the most convenient method available for checking my urine sugar level. I didn't know if my actual blood sugar was running high or low, but it was probably high most of the time. Having no hypos was the only good thing about running high blood sugar. I was so accustomed to running high that I did not notice anything peculiar. That was my perpetual state of being. If I was high there was nothing I could do. There was no fast acting insulin like Humalog available then. One injection of my beef and pork insulin in the morning, and that was it.

My teaching that summer was very successful. The experience enabled me to lose some of my shyness. Teaching again was not what I wanted to do after graduate school, but teaching wasn't so bad! How about that!

The old Chevy that Daddy let me use while going to college was holding up very well, but I wanted to buy a car of my very own. I walked three blocks down the street from the college to a local Oldsmobile dealership. There was a new light blue Oldsmobile Cutlass there. That was the one I wanted! It was expensive, but my Fellowship was so generous that there was money left over from my first year of graduate work. There was enough to make a down payment, and I took out a loan and bought that car.

I told my students at the end of summer school that they could call me at home (my parent's home). They could get their grades and not have to wait so long for report cards to be released. One of the students who called me was Lucille. I called her Lucy. Cute little thing! She made an A in both Calc I and Calc II that summer. She had the highest grade in both classes. I gave her the exam grade and course grade and then we talked for awhile. It was so easy to talk to her and she made me feel so confident and at ease. I asked her for a date. She was only three years younger than me. She was happy to go out with me. We made a date, and after hanging up, it occurred to me that my next date with Linda was on the same day. I called Linda and said I was too busy finishing summer school. It was unusual for me to lie like that, but I was really looking forward to dating Lucy!!!

Lucy had been a straight A student throughout elementary and high school. She also had all A's for her first two years at Roanoke College. She did not have to study hard at all. A very smart cookie! She was a chemistry major. Virginia Tech was only one hour from my home in Roanoke, but I stayed in Blacksburg during the week, and drove home late in the afternoon on Friday's. After starting my second year of graduate work, I was much more interested in Lucy than my studies. Lucy kept my spirits up and gave me confidence in myself. She told me I was a good teacher, considering it was my first teaching experience. She thought I ought to consider making teaching my profession.

I had never known a young lady who was so intelligent, but she was very sweet and kind. She made me feel so comfortable. We dated Friday evening, Saturday and Sunday almost every week during the fall, winter and spring until my graduation from Tech in June of 1963. It did not take long until I realized that I was in love with Lucy. I was 23 and she was the first girl I had ever kissed, and kissed and kissed...

Since my only daily insulin injection was before breakfast,

60

and there was no testing of blood sugar back then, it was easy to go on a date without letting my girlfriends know about my diabetes. I don't remember ever telling Linda, even when we ate together. Avoiding things containing sugar, but eating all the other things I wanted, never seemed to arouse any suspicion. Desserts were totally off my list when eating out . Lucy was so different and I felt so relaxed with her, so I told her about my diabetes. She was very interested. We went on a few picnics, and she baked a pie sweetened with saccharin when we did that. I still hated grad school but Lucy kept me happy and our relationship enabled me to coast through that year without much frustration. I barely made a B average again when the spring semester was over.

Writing a thesis for my MS degree was required. Its title was "An Analysis of Some Aspects of Population Projection". I won't bother you with the details of that. Aren't you glad? An oral exam was the final step to being approved for my MS degree. What a nerve racking experience! Several teachers in the Statistics Dept. and one teacher from the math department asked me questions about my thesis. My presentation did not go well at all.

I left the room feeling I had flunked. Less than thirty minutes later my advisor told me I had passed because they really liked my thesis. The orals were of secondary importance and they certainly knew I was very nervous during my presentation. I was overjoyed!!! The next day the department head told me that my Fellowship would be for only half as much if I pursued a PhD. That was actually music to my ears. Trying for a PhD was not something I wanted and this announcement gave me an easy way of escaping from grad school. It felt good to leave that behind me.

Since my summer school teaching experience had gone

well, I decided to look for a teaching position at nearby colleges for my first full time job. There was one opening that required someone who would teach both math and statistics. Lucy and I drove north to Bridgewater, Virginia one Saturday during April of that year. The president of Bridgewater College, and his wife, interviewed me and off ered me a job. My salary would be $5,000 for one school year. I thanked them and went back to my car and told Lucy I was offered a job. We went to a nice restaurant to celebrate after driving two hours back to Roanoke. I had also been hired for a second year of summer teaching at Roanoke College that year.

Lucy and my parents attended my graduation at Tech in early June, 1963. Carl, my old friend from my neighborhood, graduated there that year with a BS degree.

Graduation , MS Degree, VA Tech, June, 1963

The day after graduation Lucy and I had a date. When I took her home she told me that was our last date. I was dumbfounded and felt numb all over! This was totally unexpected. She intended on spending that summer in

Tennessee in a summer program for top ranked undergraduate chem majors. We would not be able to see each other. When I was at Bridgewater that fall she would be in her senior year at Roanoke College. She thought it was time for us to break off our relationship. She wished me well and walked into her house without looking back. She would not let me kiss her good bye.

On my way home I felt that she had dated me in order to encourage me to finish graduate school and keep me going until I graduated. I cannot help but think that way. She seemed to enjoy our dates, but any kind of permanent relationship between us was not meant to be. She realized that, but I was blinded by my love for her and wanted to spend the rest of my life with her. In many ways she was more mature than me. After a sleepless night, I told my parents what had happened. The expression on Mother's face was easy to read. She was happy about the breakup. She knew that Lucy was not the girl for me. She had told me that several times. It always made me mad.

My teaching was not very good for the first few weeks that summer. I called Linda and we resumed dating. Finally, I concentrated more on my teaching and things were going more smoothly. All in all, I had another good experience teaching that summer. Lucy was very much on my mind, she had meant so much to me. Our breaking up made me angry for awhile, but then I realized she had given me a lift whenever I needed her. She saw me through all my rough spots for nine months. I will always be very grateful to her.

Many years later I was looking at a Roanoke College alumni directory and I immediately looked for Lucy. She was married and was employed as a chemist by Eli Lilly in Indianapolis. That is the company that makes the insulin that many of us take. Is this a small world or what? I couldn't believe it. She was such an intelligent lady that I would not be at all surprised if she had a hand in the development of some of the modern day insulins. She may still be helping me even now, if that is the case. I gained 57 pounds on modern day insulins. Should I blame Lucy for that??? Nahhh! I want to have good thoughts about her, forever.

CHAPTER 8....Full Time Teaching, My True Love, Our Marriage

In August of 1963 I moved out of my parent's home and set up a room at a lady's house in Bridgewater, Va. She was an elderly lady and a substitute dorm mother and she was living there by herself. I was free to use the kitchen and watch TV. All that for $75 per month.

In early September of that year I was 24 and started teaching full time at Bridgewater College. There were no complications with my 18 years of diabetes, even though I ran high blood sugar so much of the time. I was still using Tes-Tape for testing my urine. A little urine placed on the strip of tape would make it turn various shades of green. The tape was initially yellow and if it remained yellow after inserted in urine there was 0% sugar present. If there was sugar the tape turned green. The darker the shade of green, the higher the urine sugar. I used that type of urine testing for many years. There were occasional changes and improvements in the beef/pork insulin I was using, but it was still insulin from pigs and cows. It kept me alive and I had a good life and good health despite my high blood sugar levels.

Teaching was going reasonably well that fall but it was much more challenging because I had a full schedule of five classes. It was very different from the summer school teaching. The head of the math department, who was about 5 years older than me, was dating one of the coeds on campus. Teachers were permitted to date students as long as the students were not members of their own classes. There was another young male teacher who was not at all good looking, but he was dating a very attractive female student. I thought "Hey, if they can do it so can I!!!"

The 1963 college yearbook had some good looking

prospects. I started with the senior class and made a list. Bridgewater College was a small college then and had less than 700 students. I shared an office with the head of the physics department and he knew many of the female students on campus, at least by reputation. He looked at my list and immediately said no to all of the seniors on the list. They were either married, engaged, or had questionable reputations. The dorm mother where I was staying agreed with him. Oh well, on to the junior class.

There was one very attractive gal named Jeanine. She was a junior and a physics major. My office mate knew her well. She was much like Lucy, very intelligent, a straight A student and had a good reputation. I called her that evening and we had our first date on Friday of that week. She agreed to date on Fridays only, so I called her "my girl Friday", like in the book "Robinson Crusoe". She wanted to get a PhD in nuclear physics. She was a very interesting gal, but I saw no real future in our relationship.

My girl friends had been very pretty and very intelligent, with great reputations. Why was I able to get dates with such wonderful young ladies? I found out later on that dating a teacher was a really big deal among the girls in the dorms there. It seemed that there was a good chance of getting dates with many girls on campus. Back to the yearbook. Let's see, one for Saturday, one for Sunday,....... Can you tell I had delusions of grandeur?

I had more juniors and some sophomores in a list in my little black book. The dorm mother where I was staying looked very carefully at my list and said "date this one". Her name was Anita. The dorm mother told me Anita was wonderful and I should forget about the others. That was not my plan, but I agreed to give Anita a call. After a few dates with Anita I was not so interested in calling any more girls. It was just Anita and Jeanine. I dated Jeanine on

66

Friday and Anita on Saturday, Sunday, Monday,...... the dorm mother had hit the nail on the head. Anita was different, in a very positive way. She was beautiful and so sweet.

I felt very comfortable with Anita, like I had with Lucy. I looked for that little black book one day, and it was gone. I have wondered if the dorm mother had cleaned my room and saw my list and threw it away??? She really did like Anita. I DID TOO!!! I stopped dating Jeanine. Anita and I were going steady. Anita eventually told me that the girls at her dorm had helped her fix her hair and pick out the dress she wore before our first date. I think the whole campus knew we were dating. At that stage I was even dating her on Fridays. Dating every day of the week. I wonder if any other couple ever did that. HMMM!

Anita, High School senior, 1962

Anita went home with me for the Thanksgiving weekend.
Mother loved Anita! Daddy did too! Hey, this is getting
serious here!!! Anita and I had already admitted our love
for each other. When the semester was over I went home
for Christmas and Anita went to her home in NE Virginia
to be with her family. It was agreed that I would go to
Anita's house the day after Christmas so I could meet her
family. Late on Christmas Day a terrific snow storm hit
Roanoke. The roads were plowed late the next morning, but
the driveway at our house had about 18 inches of snow on
it. My parents insisted that I stay home and wait to see my
sweetie when the spring semester began. They were out of
their minds!!! I shoveled the driveway and packed my car
while Mother was screaming at me.

Starting up the hill on our driveway was impossible. Too much ice, it was bitter cold. My tires were spinning and Daddy helped me put chains on the rear wheels. It was still impossible to make it up that hill. I was about to give up when I saw Daddy coming with his tractor. He pulled my car up the hill to the road and off I went. The roads between Roanoke and Falls Church were slick and dangerous but nothing was going to stop me. It took me about six hours, normally it would have been four hours. I found her house and met her parents and her brother. Nice people!

That evening we went downstairs to the recreation room where there was a fireplace, all warm and cozy. I proposed marriage that evening and she said yes!!! HURRAY! Months later, her Mother said she knew that we were engaged, she could tell by Anita's grin as we walked up the steps. We were going to keep it secret for a while because we had been dating for less than two months, but they knew. We planned our wedding for May 31, 1964. We were married after 7 months of courting. We celebrated our 45'th anniversary on May 31, 2009. We have had a wonderful marriage, still going strong!!!

Our Wedding, May 31, 1964

CHAPTER 9....Job Problems and The Births Of Our Children

After our marriage ceremony on May 31, 1964, we drove away and left all our parents and siblings standing there waving at us. We drove a mile or so and we realized that we did not ask for our marriage certificate. I thought that might be important, so we turned around and went back for it. The minister who married us was a Dean at the college and the son of the dorm mother who was responsible for our getting together. I told her that if the marriage did not work out I would know whom to blame. She said she was not worried. She was a very sweet lady.

Her son signed the marriage certificate and we were off to Niagara Falls. I had seen the falls previously but Anita hadn't. It is one of my favorite places. We loved it there and our honeymoon was great! I cannot remember anything we did there, except see the falls. There must have been something else too. We were there several days. My memory is failing me. Hmmmm!

That summer I was scheduled to teach for the third time at Roanoke College. That gave Anita a chance to really get to know my parents, my sister and other relatives. They all loved Anita! When the summer session ended we drove back to Bridgewater and I started my second year of full-time teaching. We were living upstairs in a three room apartment that had no air conditioning. It was miserable until the cooler weather arrived.

My teaching that year was fair. Making teaching my permanent profession was still not my intention. Anita fit in very well with the faculty wives at functions she attended. Some of the wives had been her teachers and it seemed strange to her being a member of the faculty wives group. That was my last year at Bridgewater since I lacked the

Ph.D. that was needed for tenure status.

In the years that followed I taught three years at Wingate College in NC. During that time Anita was told she was pregnant with our first child, a boy. That winter she slipped on the ice on the front steps of our apartment and hit the base of her spine on the brick step surface. Our son David Lee Vaughn was born on September 21, 1966. Anita was OK and our son was OK. I was the only male child with my last name who could continue our branch of our family tree, so having a boy was wonderful. We were so happy and everything was perfect. We were ,however, unhappy with the area in which we were living. I was also very unhappy with the college and my teaching there. We decided we should move to a new location.

My Parent's Home in Roanoke, 1967

We left Wingate in 1968 and moved to Richmond, VA. I taught two years at Virginia Commonwealth University. My second son, Gary, was born in Richmond on Sept. 9, 1969. During the delivery forceps were used. They left

72

terrible looking sores on the sides of Gary's head. We were very worried about that but the sores healed and Gary was OK.

While we were living in Richmond I found a specialist in diabetes listed in the yellow pages. He was not an endocrinologist. It was 1970 and there may not have been endos at that time, at least not in the areas where I lived. Seeing a diabetes expert seemed to be a great idea and I had high expectations. His office was very crowded and patients were spending, on the average, about 15 minutes with him. He saw me for the first time and looked at my blood test results. His lab technician had taken blood samples when I first arrived at his office complex. He frowned and said my blood sugar was very high. I do not remember the level now.

He spent so little time with me even though it was my first visit. He gave me a book about diabetes that had been written about 20 years earlier. I am almost certain it was written in the 1950's. I do not remember the author or title of the book. He told me to pay particular attention to a certain page.

That was a very strange doctor visit, very short, and not at all informative. I was very disappointed. I liked my previous GP's better than this so-called expert. I went to my car and immediately turned to the page he felt was so important. There was a chart on that page. In the leftmost column there was a list of ages at time of diagnosis, and in the adjacent column there was a prediction of age at time of death. According to that chart I was supposed to die in my late 40's. My age was 30 at that time so this suggested I had less than 20 years to live. I was terribly depressed!

I went home and showed Anita and she hugged me. She gave me the comfort I desperately needed, but that chart nagged me terribly for many years after that day. We discussed the office visit, the doctor and the book. We decided I would not see the doctor again. We threw the book in the trash can. My urine tests showed high sugar almost all the time, but I felt so good. My having no complications made it seem very unlikely that my death could be so close at hand. We wanted to believe that I was different and the statistics in that book did not apply to me. Actually, that did turn out to be the case, but we did not know that at the time. It was merely wishful thinking.

I left VCU after two years because of my not having a PhD. My uncle in Roanoke called me a gypsy math professor. It was time to find a place where I could get tenure and stop all that moving around. I looked high and low. All college teaching positions available required a PhD. Even the community colleges in Virginia required a PhD for tenure.

Time was running out when I discovered that the community colleges of New York required only an MS degree. There was a job opening at Ulster County Community College near Kingston, NY. I got the job and we moved to Kingston, NY in August of 1970.

CHAPTER 10....New York!

It was August of 1970 and Anita and I were in Kingston, NY, far from familiar surroundings in Virginia. People talked so differently! We walked into a little shop and the young woman at the counter asked "Can I help youse?" What did she say? I thought "youse" might be like a plural for "you". So two you's would be youse. We had never heard that word before.

Kingston is a small city of about 30,000 people and it was the first capitol of NY state. It was burned to the ground during the Revolutionary War, but was rebuilt in later years. The present day capitol is Albany, NY and is located 50 miles north of Kingston. Kingston is a very historic city. Reenactments of the burning of Kingston are held in the fall and people come from all over to watch the spectacle. People dressed in colonial garb and carrying old muskets and the British storming the mock village in their bright red coats all make an interesting display.

We were very hesitant about moving to New York. I had always heard southerners say that the people in New York were unfriendly and cold, and we would not like it there. Nothing could be further from the truth. People in Ulster County and the surrounding regions were very friendly and wonderful.

Teaching in a NY college was very different and challenging. The students had a much better high school background than most of my students in the southern colleges. Back then the high schools in the north were typically given higher ratings than those in southern states. My fringe benefits package in NY was vastly superior to what I had in the south. In all the colleges in which I taught in the south the fringe benefits were very poor and almost nonexistent.

During the beginning weeks of my first year teaching at that college, there was a strike by the teaching staff. This was unbelievable! The best salary and fringe benefits I had ever imagined and the faculty wanted more, along with higher salaries. I could not relate to any of it.

After explaining my feelings to my fellow faculty members, they seemed to understand. Classes were not held while faculty picketed in front of the college. I watched but did not participate in the picket lines. Some of the faculty members were arrested and jailed for one day. The community college is a state college and striking by faculty is illegal in NY State. I was sorry for my friends who spent the night in jail.

After a week or so the bargaining between the faculty and the county ended. Fringe benefits were even better and there were faculty wage increases of 20% retroactive for the preceding year, and another 20% for the year in progress. The faculty won at the bargaining table, big time! I got the benefit of the raise for the current year and that was a big bonus for my family. Not participating in the strike in any way made me feel somewhat guilty though. If a faculty in a southern college even talked about striking, heads would roll, and it would never take place. Things were certainly different in northern states.

Teaching at the community college was very enjoyable. I made many wonderful friends there and became a popular teacher. My students would sometimes laugh at my southern accent, but I eventually lost most of it through the years. I will always have some of that accent. There is an old saying, "You can take an old boy outta the south but you can't take the south outta the boy".

In early 1973 there was a light snow and I left campus early that day because of a doctor's appointment in Kingston. There were about two inches of snow on the roads. After starting north on route 209 I saw a car stalled at the bottom of the hill. The driver was trying to move forward, but the car's wheels were spinning. The tires on that car were probably not snow tires, even though they were required by NY State law during the winter.

I was moving along at 35 miles per hour, the posted speed limit, but I needed to slow down to avoid hitting that car ahead of me. My car started sliding and it was very difficult staying in my lane. The sliding caused my car to move much faster. I turned toward the right shoulder of the road to avoid a collision with the other car. There was a steep slope there and my car went down the hill, knocking down a road sign and a few young trees.

I was not hurt but my car was damaged. A NY State trooper showed up a few minutes later. It was snowing hard and he had me get in his car with him while he made his written report. Freezing rain had fallen before the snow started, but I was teaching in a cozy building while all that was happening. The ice had caused my car to slide, and the accident resulted. The trooper said I was driving too fast for the road conditions involved. He did not give me a ticket, maybe he thought I had been through enough.

My blood sugar must have been low because I was shaking while sitting in the trooper's car. Maybe it was just the accident itself that left me shaking. Testing my urine sugar was impossible under the circumstances. I always had to guess whether my blood sugar was low at times like this. I missed my doctor's appointment that day. A wreck truck pulled my car up the steep hill to the road the following day. The frame on the front of the car was badly damaged and the repair would cost me more than the car was worth.

We were struggling financially when I went out the next day to buy another car. It had to be a cheap one. Friends of mine had much trouble with their used cars and I wanted a new car. There was a Ford dealership near my home and I went there and bought a 1972 Ford Pinto Wagon. It was a small car and not very expensive. Our checking account was almost wiped out when I made the down payment on the Pinto. That summer Anita was learning to drive. She had been learning for a few years but she never had a driver's license. She got her license a few weeks before we started a trip south to visit our parents in Virginia that August.

There was a funny rattling or clinking sound beneath the car. We stopped in Newburgh at a Ford dealership not long after we started our trip. They said the shock absorbers needed replacing. The car was only five months old and I was very suspicious, but I had them do the work. We continued the trip, but we started hearing the clinking noise again. We assumed everything was OK since the mechanics had given the car a thorough inspection.

When we got to Stroudsburg, PA I asked Anita to take over the driving. We had planned for her to do some of the driving that day. We were headed west on Interstate 80 out of Stroudsburg. Anita was passing a slow moving trailer truck when she said that the steering was not working. She had almost passed the trailer when our car started veering to our right. She turned the steering wheel to the left, but the car did not respond. The steering was shot.

Our car entered the lane to our right immediately ahead of the trailer. The driver turned the trailer sharply to his left to avoid hitting our car head on. The impact caused our car to spin around 180 degrees and tore the back end off. Our two boys were 6 and 3 years old. We had folded the back seat of the wagon down, and the boys had been playing on the platform there near the luggage we had packed for the trip. They were not thrown from the car but David, our oldest, was bleeding from his mouth.

Anita was shaking and we were all in shock but none of us seemed to be seriously hurt. David was bleeding from his mouth but his teeth were intact. The driver had stopped a few hundred feet ahead and he walked back to see if we were hurt. We told him we were OK. He said he had never been in an accident since he started driving his trailer. We told him our steering was shot and we could not control our car. The police arrived and we were treated very nicely. No ticket was issued and the policeman took us to a motel nearby. We checked into the motel for the night. We called our parents and told them what happened. A little later the policeman took us to the garage nearby where our car had been taken. We gathered the remaining things we had left in the car. I noticed that the garage was owned by the Ford motor company, but did not think much about it at that time.

That evening Anita said her neck was hurting badly. We called a cab and went to the ER at a nearby hospital. Anita had a bad whiplash and was given a cervical collar. The next day a friend from the college drove to our motel and took us home to Kingston.

We read an article in the Kingston newspaper which said that many Pintos were being recalled. A metal sleeve had not been installed on those cars beneath the steering column. The article stated that a small pebble or rock could bounce from the road surface and lodge itself in the exposed steering column, causing the steering to fail. We felt that was exactly what had happened to us. That would explain the clinking noise we had heard. I called the garage in Stroudsburg and told them what we had read. They said they knew nothing about the article. It had been only a few days since we had the accident but we were told the car had been put through the crusher.

I had told them about the steering having failed when we were there at their garage. During our phone conversation they said they found nothing wrong with the steering. I felt that they were lying, but what could I do? When we were at that garage they said we did not owe them anything for the towing if we agreed to sign the car over to them. We took our car tags and left. We did that, thinking it was a good deal.

We needed another car but we could not afford one. We called Anita's father and he sent us a down payment by money order. I bought a new Dodge Dart only five months after I had bought the Pinto. We made our trip to Virginia later that month. The car drove like a dream. Our parents were so happy to see us! Anita still had a sore neck and she was not able to turn her head without experiencing pain.

When we got back home Anita was having terrible pain and we went to our doctor. He said she would have to have nerve block surgery in her neck so she could turn her head without having all that pain. The doctor did the surgery in his office. He numbed the right side of her neck and then stuck a very long needle deep inside. He twirled the needle around to sever the damaged nerves. A few days after the surgery she was turning her head and the pain was much better. After a few weeks the pain was gone. The nerve block procedure was a complete success.

In the months that followed we talked about that terrible ordeal. We still thought that metal sleeve not being installed on the Pinto caused the accident. We could have been killed. I think our being in good physical condition after the accident and the surgery being so successful, kept us from being so bitter. We were so grateful to be safe at home and our health was good. We had to put that behind us, but it was very difficult to do so. In the years ahead we had awful feelings every time we passed the Ford dealership where we bought that Pinto.

David & Gary 1970

Hmmm! Was moving to NY the right thing to do??

CHAPTER 11....My Wife, My Caretaker

Anita was born in Washington, D. C. in May, 1944. She lived with her parents and younger brother in Falls Church Virginia. I was teaching at Bridgewater College when Anita was a sophomore there, and we started dating in November, 1963. She knew nothing about diabetes when we were dating and none of her relatives or family members had diabetes. She learned many things about my diabetes, but she never worried about me. There was very little reason for her to worry, since I almost always had high blood sugar. She did not see me have a hypo while we were dating.

We were married in May, 1964, when Anita was 20. She began to learn how to cook for me. It was not really that difficult. She used artificial sweeteners and never put any sugar in anything she prepared for me. There was really no advice being given by my doctors about diabetes care, so I ate any food I wanted, as long as it did not contain a significant amount of sugar.

There were a few hypos soon after we were married. One of them occurred one day while walking back to our upstairs apartment near the college and my vision became very blurred. For some reason I was not aware it was a hypo. It came on very fast and I was in a fog. Making it up the steps was very difficult for me. I was out of breath and my heart was beating terribly fast. Anita recognized my symptoms and fed me sugar. That may have been the first time she had to bring me out of a hypo.

Urine testing was a very poor substitute for a glucometer. When there was high sugar in my urine it could have been because I had not passed any urine for several hours. The sugar in the urine may have been from another part of the day. There were many times that my urine tests did not indicate that my blood sugar was low, but it actually was. Anita became very good at detecting my restlessness during the night. She would usually wake me before my blood sugar dropped too low, but in some cases, she would have to feed me sugar. It was rare for me to experience unconsciousness with a hypo during our first years of marriage.

After we moved to New York there were a few times that we could not pay all our bills on time and Anita took a job at Sears. Another year she was the Assistant Director of the local Red Cross. They were low salaried jobs, but we needed the money and her working helped very much.

In 1977 I finally had a doctor who knew a lot about diabetes. Then in the late 1980s I learned about the importance of low carb dieting. Applying this new knowledge greatly improved my control and I did not have high blood sugar so frequently. Becoming more accustomed to lower blood sugar helped very much, but there were more frequent hypos. There was at least one bad one each week. When the hypos occurred more frequently Anita was very good about it. She did a great job! I praised her every time she brought me out of a hypo.

Anita devoted much of her time to our two sons. In the 1980s the boys were in high school and demanded much less of her time. She was a stay-at-home mom and she had more time on her hands. The boys went off to college and the two of us were alone. It was a very different life style without our children at home. I was still teaching for the next ten years, until my retirement in 1997. Anita took over the lawn care and made our backyard very beautiful with her handiwork. She planted many flowers and did much wonderful landscaping. It was a work of art.

In the early 1980s we decided we needed mortgage insurance on our home. A local insurance company required a physical examination. A very old semi retired doctor had me fill out a form. He asked me for a urine sample. He tested the urine with the special tape used for that purpose and it turned a dark green. That indicated high urine sugar. He said he could not recommend me for mortgage insurance based on that urine test. How could he make that decision based on a single urine test? He walked outside with me and we stood by my car. At that time I had been diabetic for about 35 years. He told me that I was very lucky to have lived so long without complications. He went on to say he had known another male diabetic like me who was doing very well, but had high urine sugar almost all the time. Less than one year after he had seen the man, he developed kidney failure and was going blind because of his diabetes.

The doctor told me I should not depend on living much longer. This reminded me of the doctor in Richmond, who did not expect me to live beyond my 40s. This doctor had very antiquated ideas.

The next day Metropolitan Life Insurance sounded more promising. They called Dr. B. and learned that I was doing very well after 35 years of diabetes, and there were no complications. They offered me a mortgage insurance policy and we also got one for Anita. Metropolitan was a good choice. The insurance policies gave us peace of mind. We never had to use them. Our house was fully paid for in August of 1995.

David was born , 1966

Our Family, 1974

Shirley was a caregiver on many occasions before I left home and started teaching. She would hear me at night from her bedroom, if my restlessness during my sleep awakened her. She was kind of tuned in to me when I was having a bad hypo. She woke my parents several times when they were sleeping too soundly to hear me. She did this during my high school and undergraduate college years.

As previously mentioned, Mother had been calling Dr. D. and telling him what she wanted him to tell me before my appointments with him. She also told Shirley to go places with me, when I had intended to go alone. Shirley used to ask if she could go to movies with me. We loved each other and we enjoyed being with each other, but it seemed somewhat peculiar that she would want to see the horror and science fiction movies. It was not her kind of entertainment. She also wanted to go fishing with me several times. I was not dating while in high school and movies and fishing were two of my favorite pastimes. Mother feared I would have a hypo while going out alone, so she asked Shirley to go with me. This completely fooled me and Shirley did not tell me about it until many, many years later. It surprised me when she told me, but it made sense because that was just like Mother. It made me feel bad for Shirley. She says she enjoyed the movies and the fishing trips, but she was actually doing this for Mother and for me. Shirley was, and still is, a wonderful sister and a wonderful human being.

Anita and I were married in May, 1964, and Shirley and her boyfriend, Don, were married two months later in July. The wedding was held in the living room at our home in Roanoke. Here is a picture of my beautiful sister.

Shirley Vaughn Rhodes, 1964

My Sister's Daughter, Debbie, and Her Family, 2009

CHAPTER 12....My Parents, Their Later Years

Daddy was a wonderful provider for our family. I have never known a man to work so hard. He had a lot of muscle and he worked our little farm just like he had worked farms before he was married. He also worked a 40 hour week at the Roanoke post office and planted shrubbery at people's houses, while working for Mother's uncle. He was a very kind and honest man and he did favors for his parents, siblings and neighbors.

Mother was also a very hard worker, but she had many health problems that bothered her when Shirley and I were children. Asthma and very bad varicose veins gave her a lot of trouble. She still managed to work hard on our farm, canning hundreds of quarts of vegetables and fruit, helping tend the very large garden, doing the house work and being a wonderful Mother to Shirley and me. She watched me and cared for me the only way she could after I was diagnosed with diabetes. She stopped having trouble with her asthma and varicose veins when she was older and then her health was very good. My parents made a wonderful team and Shirley and I were so lucky to have both of them.

My parents and most of my relatives were very religious people. All of my grandparents and several of my aunts and uncles belonged to the Primitive Baptist churches in the southern Virginia area. That may be a Christian denomination with which you are unfamiliar. It is characterized by no music in the church, no Sunday school, no choir, just very plain and simple. The preachers are not called ministers, and they do not go to college to become preachers. The preachers feel the call from God and they know that is their duty.

People who join have some kind of sign, such as a dream,

that makes it clear to them that God wants them to join the church. At the conclusion of a Sunday meeting a prospective member will walk down the aisle to the front of the church and announce that he/she wants to join. That person is usually very emotional and find it difficult to speak. A discussion usually follows and the people may hear what made this person know that joining was the proper thing to do that day. If the member is accepted, then there is great rejoicing.

Daddy had this experience several years before he died. We were living far away and I did not know he was going to join. He didn't either, until the preacher was about done for the day. Daddy became very weak and was shaking as he walked down the aisle. He explained why he knew he was supposed to join that day. He was accepted and he was changed in many ways after that day. He was baptized in the baptismal pond on the church grounds. The banks of the pond were lined with well wishers. It is a very joyous occasion when a Primitive Baptist member is baptized.

Daddy had made the two acres immediately surrounding our house very beautiful by planting many wonderful shrubs that had grown very large. He was gifted at landscaping and the large yard was a virtual show place. Mother's large flower gardens added to the beauty of the place. People would stop and want to take pictures of the landscape. The magnolia trees had become quite large and were beautiful to see. On one occasion, a wedding party stopped and got my parent's permission to have their pictures taken on the grounds. Most of their property had been sold and the back seven acres became part of a country club and golf course.

Several years later Daddy started having pains in his chest. The doctor told him he had a weak heart valve and that it should be replaced with a pig's heart valve. Daddy felt that

94

God would take care of him and surgery was unnecessary. Mother begged him to have the surgery. He finally gave in and the surgery was scheduled to take place in approximately three weeks.

In the spring of 1983 there was a bad drought in the Roanoke area and some of the beautiful shrubbery was turning brown. Daddy had a lot of muscle and he would carry a five gallon bucket of water in each hand. He carried those buckets up the hill from the back yard water source to the front yard, to water his boxwoods. The shrubs were so important to him that he wanted to continue watering them, despite his heart problem. We were visiting my parents at that time and I begged him to stop. I have never had much muscle and he would not let me help. He felt that God would protect him. If he died then God wanted it that way. He seemed to be OK when we left and went home.

On Mother's Day that year Daddy was sleeping, while lying back in his recliner in the den. Mother was watching TV. She looked over at Daddy and he suddenly made a little gasping noise and stopped breathing. He died in his sleep. He died a few days before his scheduled heart surgery. Mother grieved long and hard. There were many people including Primitive Baptist church members at his funeral. There were relatives there whom I had not seen in so many years. The funeral was on a Wednesday and we stayed through Saturday and returned home Sunday. I had to return to my teaching and there was no substitute to replace me at the college.

Mother had thought for so long that God might give her a sign that she should join the church, but it never happened. One of her brothers became a Primitive Baptist preacher and. He still preaches in the south central Virginia area.

Mother lived alone after that. She was very healthy, so that did not seem to be a problem. She rode her riding mower and mowed her three acre lawn. Shirley and her husband looked after Mother and made sure she was in good shape. It made me feel very guilty that my home in New York was so far from Roanoke. I wanted to help take care of Mother, but my teaching position made it impossible. We visited Mother twice each year, just like we had done before Daddy died.

In April, 2000, Mother was diagnosed with a tumor growing inside her head, beneath her brain. It was very near her brain, but not touching it. The tumor was not cancer. The surgeon in Roanoke told Mother and Shirley that it would be a dangerous if she were to have it removed. Her age was a factor. He said that installing a shunt to drain the fluid off her brain would probably enable her to live about five more years. Mother was not able to understand everything that was said and she did not hear that she might have only five years left. She had the surgery to install the shunt in May of 2000, and that really helped some of her symptoms. Shirley and Don had to keep a close watch on her for her remaining years. Mother gradually became more and more feeble during the years that followed, even though the tumor did not appear to be growing. A few years after her diagnosis she was taken to a nearby nursing home in Roanoke. She liked the nursing home and she made friends with other people living there. She used a walker and made trips on her own to the dining room on the first floor.

In early 2005 she started falling, even though she used her walker. Both she and her walker would topple over. She was hospitalized several times due to falls and her health was declining. The first few times this happened she was not hurt badly. One day in May, 2005, she had a bad fall and hurt her head, causing terrible bruising on her face. We talked on the phone one evening and she told me she was ready to die. She said life was not worth living anymore. The next day she died in her sleep, just like Daddy had done. We went to her funeral and it seemed like a replay of Daddy's funeral 22 years earlier. I saw the same relatives and friends again. It seemed like I saw them only at funerals.

My parents had a wonderful marriage and a good life. Their home and property were sold in 2007. Passing by my old home place is very difficult now. I want so much to stop and go inside the house, but someone else lives there now. I will never get to go inside the house again.

Shirley and I have many wonderful memories of Mother and Daddy, and we talk frequently about our happy times with them.

Shirley, Mother, Richard 1990s

CHAPTER 13.... Diabetes History and My History Prior to 1980

Hesy-Ra, an Egyptian physician, recognized frequent urination (polyuria) as a symptom among his patients in 1552 B.C. That was more than 3500 years ago and it is considered to be the earliest known record of diabetes.

In the first century AD a Greek physician, Arateus, used the term "diabetes" which comes from the Greek word for "siphon". He described diabetes as "the melting down of flesh and limbs into urine". Until the 11'th century diabetes was sometimes diagnosed by "water tasters" who drank some of the patient's urine. If the urine was sweet-tasting, it was thought that diabetes was present. The present day phrase "diabetes mellitus" is derived from the word "mellitus", the Latin word for honey.

Treatments for diabetics before insulin was discovered have always interested me. In 1500 BC a diet of fruits, grain and honey was recommended to reduce excessive urination. In the first century AD Arateus recommended "oil of roses, dates, raw quinces and gruel."

In 230 BC Paul of Aegina thought that the dehydration experienced by diabetes patients was caused by weakness in the kidneys. The remedy he prescribed consisted of "pot-herbs, endive, lettuce, rock fishes, juices of knot grass, elecampane in dark colored wine, dates and myrtle" to be used in the early stages of diabetes. That was followed by a mixture of "vinegar, rose oil and navel-wort", applied as a poultice spread on the skin over the kidneys. He also permitted cutting of veins, or bleeding, to help diabetics.

When I read the contents of some of the remedies from so long ago, I can't help but think of tales of witches, and their brews for casting spells on their victims.

In 1000 AD Greek physicians prescribed "exercise, emetics and sudorifics". All diuretics and drugs were to be avoided.

Prior to the 11'th century there was really no knowledge of how to treat diabetes. Children died very quickly with it. Older people lived longer, but they suffered greatly with terrible complications before dying.

In the 17'th century there were doctors who prescribed "gelly of viper's flesh, broken red coral, sweet almonds and fresh flowers of blind nettles". The tasting of urine was still being used to diagnose diabetes. This method continued until the 20'th century.

There were two schools of thought in the 17'th century. One theory proposed replacing the sugar lost in the urine by following a diet high in carbohydrates. The second school believed that **carbohydrates should be restricted to reduce excess sugar. EUREKA!!! That may have been the first time excessive carbohydrates were considered as detrimental to diabetics.** The first theory seemed to be much more popular, and the idea of restricting carbohydrates seems to have been lost for the next few centuries. I say that because treatments being proposed in the late 1800's included bleeding, blistering and doping, with no further reference to restriction of carbohydrates. What a shame!!! If the second school of thought had become the popular one, that may have accelerated the advancements in the years that followed.

In 1945, the year of my diagnosis, carbohydrates were never mentioned. I did not know about the effect of carbohydrates until the mid 1980's. That was about 300 years after the initial proposal that carbohydrates should be limited in a diabetic's diet.

In the late 1850's Priorry, a French physician, advised eating very large quantities of sugar. In the 1870's Bouchardat, another French physician, prescribed individualized diets for his diabetic patients. An Italian diabetes specialist, Catoni, locked up his patients to force them to follow their diets.

In 1910 Sharbey-Shafer in Edinburgh found that diabetics lacked a chemical in there pancreases. He called that chemical insulin.

Popular diets in the period 1900-1915 included the "oat cure", which featured eating oatmeal, the "milk diet", the "rice cure" , "potato therapy" and even the use of opium.

Insulin was discovered in 1921 by Dr. Frederick Banting and Charles Best at the University of Toronto. Thank goodness for the Canadians!!! The first insulin was taken from pigs and cows, and was impure. Large doses were necessary, and they frequently caused abscesses at the injection site. At first the beef and pork insulin was short acting, and multiple doses were needed each day.

Dr. Banting's home was in Alliston, Ontario, Canada. The pictures below show the Banting Memorial. A friend of mine visited the memorial, and sent me this picture in an email. It gave me chills when I read it. We diabetics using insulin owe him so much!!!

In 1922 Eli Lily and company was licensed to manufacture the insulin. By 1923 this short acting insulin became available to the general public. In that same year Dr. Banting and Prof. Macleod won the Nobel Prize for Medicine for their discovery of insulin. In 1925 home testing for urine sugar with Benedict's solution became widely available.

In the 1930's new types of beef and pork insulin were introduced. A longer acting insulin, PZI, was created in 1936 by a Danish researcher, Hans Christian Hagedorn. NPH insulin was available in 1938.

In 1944 the first standardized insulin syringe was introduced. It was made of glass. The needles used with that syringe had to be sterilized by boiling. The needles had to be sharpened frequently. My family lived in an area where all the residents had their own wells. Our water was "hard water", with lime, and contained material that caused a deposit to form on my needles when they were boiled. Each morning before the syringe and needle were boiled, Daddy took a whet stone and rubbed the needle against it to remove the deposit. If there was some of the deposit still left on the needle, it became very difficult to push the needle into my flesh. Injections on my arms were more painful so we usually used my upper legs. We were told to inject the insulin into muscle and my abdomen was never used in my childhood. I started giving myself my own injections when I was 12.

In 1945, the year I was diagnosed, a 10 year old child diagnosed with diabetes was not expected to live beyond the age of 45. The two doctors who examined me in 1970 and in the 1980's suggested I would die while in my 40's. It seems that they were still hanging on to that prediction made in 1945.

"The Story Of Insulin" is a must see if you use insulin. If you go to the home page of the dlife.com website and use the search option at the top of the page, you can gain access to this inspiring video. Type "history of insulin" in the box and choose the appropriates item on the following page. This presentation is frequently updated and is worth seeing again and again.

For many years after my diagnosis, I had only one doctor. I followed his advice to the letter and avoided food with a high sugar content. My blood sugar ran much too high from my diagnosis in 1945, until the 1980's, when low carb dieting entered the picture. Testing my urine sugar before eating each meal and limiting my portion sizes and types of food accordingly was my routine. Those test results, however, did not necessarily correlate well at all with my blood sugar level at any given time.

Through the years it was obvious that certain foods were not good for me. The highs I could feel were probably in the mid 200's and higher. The lows that I felt were probably in the mid 100's and lower.

Low carb meals and the glucometer gave me a whole new regimen for my diabetes management. My diabetes was under much better control in the years that followed.

Too much fruit, pasta, bread, cereal and the desserts Mother made for me made me feel high when I ate big portions. Limiting my portion sizes made me feel much better. That was a crude form of carb control, but it was helpful. We knew nothing about carbs, but we knew what foods made me run the highest blood sugar. By limiting my portion sizes when eating the troublesome foods I began feeling high blood sugar even when my blood sugar was in the upper 100's. This certainly helped me during my teen years. My weight was not a problem prior to the 1990s.

After leaving Roanoke and starting my life away from my family, I moved from place to place several times. Moving always involved looking for a new doctor, but there was never one that seemed to know much about diabetes, until the 1980's. They were OK for diagnosing and writing prescriptions and they were well suited for my wife and children, since there was no diabetes involved there. Knowledge about diabetes progressed very slowly prior to the 1980's. The testing of urine to estimate the amount of sugar in my body left a lot to be desired. All of my doctors were general practitioners and they certainly did not specialize in the treatment of diabetes. For these reasons I learned very little about diabetes during those years. Insulin was wonderful!!! It was the only thing keeping me alive.

In 1961 the first disposable insulin syringes were introduced. The pain was greatly reduced with these syringes since the diameter of the needles was smaller. I was still using my glass syringe, and the old thick needles for several years after my marriage in 1964. It seems strange that I did not know about the disposable syringes until so many years after they first became available. These syringes were wonderful. It was no longer necessary to boil the glass syringe and needles every morning in order to sterilize them for repeated use.

Urine strips were also developed in the 1960's. It was no longer necessary to put Benedict's solution and urine in a test tube and boil it on the stove. Holding the strips of tape in my urine stream, and observing the color change, gave me my urine sugar level. It was so easy to do.

During the years 1963-70, while teaching in the south, I did not see doctors about my diabetes more than twice per year. My family saw them for other reasons but my diabetes seemed to play second fiddle to ordinary illnesses, like colds and flues.

After moving to Kingston, NY, in 1970, I found a GP who had moved to this country from Germany. He was the best doctor I had had at that time. He knew much more about diabetes than any of my previous doctors, and he spent as much as 30 minutes with me on each visit. He tested my blood sugar himself while I watched. My blood sugar was usually high but his instructions enabled me to learn a little about carbs, and certain things I should eat in very limited portions. His advice helped, and before he was in semi retirement, in the late 1970's, my control had improved. My urine sugar still showed high much of the time.

In 1977 my doctor was about to retire and move out of the area. A neighbor recommended a new doctor, who had just opened up his practice. Dr. B. was from Thailand. He was a specialist in internal medicine, and his office was in the basement level of the Kingston Hospital. Dr. B. was in charge of the dialysis department at the hospital for a long time. He spent a lot of time with me on my first visit. He obviously knew much more about diabetes than any of my precious doctors had. Dr. B. is the best doctor I have ever had, and he is still my doctor today. He is only a few years younger than me, and may retire at any time. Having to do without Dr. B. will be difficult for me. He has helped me so much. He has had many diabetic patients, and they talk about him in the waiting room. Everybody loves Dr.B.

The first insulin pump was developed in 1963 by Dr. Arnold Kadish. It delivered both glucagon and insulin.

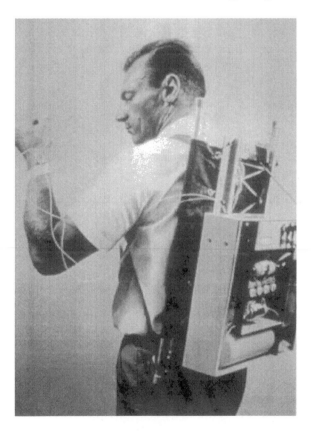

****

Reference for Chapter 13:

Sattley, Melissa. *Diabetes Health*. History of Diabetes. December 17, 2008.

CHAPTER 14....Wonderful Progress In The 1980s

The Ames reflectance meter was the first portable glucose meter (glucometer). It was introduced in 1969. They were not very popular at first because of the size and expense. Dr. Bernstein, in one of his books, described his first Ames meter: "...The instrument had a four inch-galvanometer with a jeweled bearing, weighed three pounds and, cost $650". When they became smaller and less expensive they were used more extensively.

Dr. B. told me to buy a glucometer in the early 1980's. That was the first time I had heard of one. It was the Accu-Chek meter, perhaps their first model. It was much bigger and more cumbersome to operate than today's meters, but it was certainly a big improvement when compared to the old Ames meter. It took a much longer time to show my blood sugar level. The numbers on the meter were consistently high at the beginning. Sometimes they were over 200. I did not trust or like this crazy meter! It could not possibly be correct! How could all those highs be correct? This had to be a defective meter. But no, it was not defective. It finally became obvious to me that I had been running very high blood sugar for so much of the during my first 40 years.

Dr. B. confirmed my suspicions and we talked at length about it. What a revelation! Why hadn't I developed terrible diabetic complications after 40 years of high blood sugar? Dr. B. could not answer that question and he still can't today. He told me he had other patients who had diabetes for a long time and some of them were on dialysis, or had heart or eye problems, or amputations.

Ames Glucose Meter, 1969

In the late 1980's I started logging my BG levels, insulin dosages and number of carbs eaten. It was a very new experience for me and making out those logs, and watching my control gradually improve, was very revealing. I was still using beef and pork insulin when Dr. B. became my doctor. He had me stay with that insulin for several more years.

The hemoglobin A1c test was developed in 1979. With a single blood sample the A1c test can track the average blood glucose level for a period of two to three months. My first A1c, in 1980, was 10.6. In 1981 there was an 11.8. My control kept improving but my A1c's were still too high. Dr. B. asked me to consider going to the Joslin Diabetes Center in Boston for treatment. Since my control was better, and I had no diabetes complications, I did not want to go to Boston.

The first insulin pump was also introduced in 1979, but it was inconvenient for most people because of its size. It had to be carried around in a backpack. Pumps introduced in the 1980's were smaller and more easily used. At one time in the 1980's, Dr. B. asked me to consider using an insulin pump. Again I refused his advice because my A1c's were getting better and better. He saw room for improvement and wanted me to pump. He never pressed me to make changes if he saw I was opposed. Now I wish that he had insisted that I use a pump. It would have helped me so much back then.

I have used many different insulins through the years. Beef and pork insulin was improved several times since my diagnosis. My first beef and pork insulin was NPH. that was followed by Lente in the 1950s, Humulin N and R in the 1980s, and a 75/25 Humalog mix in a pen in 1999. I don't know exactly when each of those insulins were initially prescribed. Dr. B. has been my doctor since 1977. He has always been very good about keeping up with new developments and technological advancements in order to best help his diabetes patients. It is very likely that he had me use new insulins very soon after they became available.

In 1983 Eli Lilly Corp. produced Humulin insulin which involved using human DNA. It was the first genetically engineered product cleared by the U.S. Food and Drug Administration. Humulin was an exact replica of the insulin produced in the human pancreas. Humulin-N had a duration of up to 24 hours. Humulin-R was a more rapidly acting insulin with a duration of 6 to 8 hours. I don't think it would have been possible for me to use the Humulin insulins for basal/bolus control because the duration of the Humulin R was so long. If it was injected prior to each meal using carb counting, then consecutive doses would overlap, unless the meals were 8 hours apart. In any case, I did not know anything about carb counting or basal/bolus, until the late 1990s. It was a few years after Humulin was introduced that I started following a low carb diet.

Going to a hospital emergency room with a hypo was

necessary only once during my life time. It happened in the 1980s when Anita had not been able to bring me out of my unconscious state. There were two or three other ambulance visits when the same thing occurred, but the shot they gave me each time worked so quickly that I was able to stand up immediately and walk around. I was fully aware of my surroundings, and at my request, the paramedics had me sign a paper that allowed me to stay at home.

There were times when I wished that I could go back to the beef and pork insulins. There were so few hypos with the older insulins, but there was so much high blood sugar then. It was much healthier for me to be running lower blood sugar while using the newer insulins.

While using the more advanced insulins there were occasional lows and mild hypos while teaching. There were times that my vision would get blurry. After apologizing to my students and eating sugar from my briefcase, my lecture continued with no problem. I did not want to have the reputation of a teacher whose performance in the classroom was jeopardized by my diabetes. Using separate vials of insulin and counting carbs greatly improved my control. Hypos while teaching rarely occurred.

In the 1980's, while using the Humulin insulins, I was teaching a class in basic Statistics. All students in the nursing program at the college were required to take the Statistics course. There were no other teachers at the college with a degree in Statistics, so I taught most of the Statistics classes at that time. There were many nurses in my classes through the years. One summer there were about 25 students in my Statistics class and approximately 10 of them were nurses. While walking to reach my class one evening, my vision became very blurred, and I was very dizzy. It seemed to hit me so suddenly. My container of sugar was not in my pocket. I recognized one of my students in the hall and asked him to go to the classroom and tell them that class would start late.

There was no change or one dollar bills in my pockets to use in the candy machine. My thinking was so muddled that it did not occur to me to go to the classroom, so the nurses could take care of me. I went outside to my car. The parking lot was rather dark and my vision was so bad that finding my car was very difficult. After finally finding my car, I grabbed the roll of quarters used for tolls, and headed back to the candy machine. It was not in the same building as my class. My hands were shaking and some coins dropped on the floor. My vision was so bad that I had to feel for the coin slot. A few coins fell into the slot. Reading the letters and numbers on the machine was impossible, but pushing buttons and pulling knobs caused something to drop.

It felt like a big round cookie. I wanted candy, but a big cookie with some sticky stuff between layers was fine. After gobbling it down, I headed to the other building where my students were patiently waiting. The class started about 15 minutes late. I explained what had happened and the nurses were all over me for not asking them to help. A couple of them were, perhaps, in their late 30's, and had been nurses in the local hospitals. They asked me questions to see if I was OK. They were very concerned. The class started late, but I have always bounced back from those hypos very well. The class was about 2 1/2 hours long, but considering what had happened, things actually went rather well that evening.

Two days later I had a terrible hypo during the night and Anita could not get me to eat anything. I was convulsing and she called an ambulance. It came promptly and they gave me a much needed injection of glucose and took me to the hospital. During my two days in the hospital one of the nurses from my class waited on me. Another nurse from my class kept dropping in, even though she was on duty in another part of the hospital. My hospital stay was on a weekend and I was released in time to meet with my statistics class on Monday evening. Everybody knew what had happened. That was the only time in my 34 years of teaching that I had received help from my students .

I never missed a class meeting during my 34 years of teaching because of my diabetes. My attendance while attending college classes was also perfect at the undergraduate level, but I missed one day in graduate school because of weakness from the flu. Climbing stairs to the fourth floor where my classes were held was too much for me that day. There were no elevators in that building.

Low carb dieting, glucose meters, exercising, careful logging of all my numbers and better insulins had turned my life around. There were still some hypos, but they were no longer false hypos. There were some highs, but my control was by far the best I had ever experienced. Dr. B. was my guide through all these changes. He is largely responsible for my being alive and healthy at the present time.

Our Kingston house, 1970s

Roanoke, 1970s

CHAPTER 15....My Sons, David and Gary

David was born in Monroe, NC on Sept. 21, 1966. He was a perfectly normal baby and he had a perfectly normal childhood. We had a small apartment and he had no playmates. Anita was so good with him. She was born to be a mother. David was such a sweet child and rarely woke us during the night.

Gary's birth was a bit different. We were living west of Richmond, VA, in Tukahoe Village. The village was a housing development that was built in a swampy region. Tons of soil had been used to build up the area so houses could be constructed there. Days before Gary was due to be born we had a lot of rain. The roads leading into the village were at a lower level than the village itself. Some of those roads were covered with water a few feet deep. The village had become an island. We could not drive off our island. We found that there was a doctor in the village and he agreed to deliver Gary if it was necessary. We were lucky, the rains stopped the day before Gary was born and the water was not so deep. We made it to the hospital and Gary was born on September 9,1969. There were no problems after that, but we had a few anxious hours before the rain stopped.

David and Gary were both wonderful children who never got into any trouble. There were never any substance abuse problems. They were both quiet, intelligent and well behaved children, who never caused us any problems.

I had been diabetic for twenty one years before David was born and never thought anything about taking my insulin when the boys were present. It has been so long now that I cannot remember if they were curious about me injecting. They grew up with it and it was just a part of our every day routine. I tested my urine in the bath room and there was no glucometer for my testing my blood sugar until they were in their late teens. There was very little evidence of me even being diabetic. With my having so much high blood sugar almost all the time, there were rarely any hypos while they were growing up. I must have seemed like a normal daddy with no health problems.

When we moved to New York, David was three and Gary was eleven months old. My birthday is Sept. 10, Gary's is Sept. 9 and David's is Sept. 21. Gary was three weeks premature and was almost born on my birthday.

When Gary was preschool age, we noticed that he was very bright, but there was something wrong. We could not identify the problem. He was having trouble in school. We took him to a center in Kingston where he was tested. He could not respond to written questions, but showed very high intelligence when he responded to questions given orally. We were referred to an expert in learning disabilities. Mrs. R. said that Gary had learning disabilities. She told us she could work with him and enable him to correct these problems. She worked with Gary for two years. He began making better grades in school. When he was in high school, he was such a great student that they kept yanking him out of classes and putting him in accelerated classes. He was extremely bright! Mrs. R. really knew what she was doing with Gary. We were so lucky to have the help of such an expert way back in 1976.

When David was very young he wanted to grow up and drive a fire truck. Later on he wanted to be a magician. He put on magic shows for us and his grandparents.

In 1980 I wanted to take my family out west to see Yellowstone, the Grand Canyon, Mt. Rushmore and many other interesting sites. We had a family meeting and I gave my sons a choice of the big vacation that I had explained in detail, or a computer. That was the first PC released by Apple, before IBM had released its first PC. My sons had no difficulty deciding. They wanted a computer. We were very short of spare cash and we could not afford both a vacation and a computer. If they had not chosen a computer, I wonder if their futures would have turned out differently. We were saving every bit of money that we could for their college education. Their majors in college were in computers and their lives have revolved around computers ever since. Their choice was the correct one and I am proud of them for having made it.

David did very well in school and he was also placed in advanced math and science classes. He attended the community college where I taught and thought he wanted to enter the business field. Later on he wanted to be a doctor. He made B's in both introductory business and biology courses and was discouraged. He then decided that he would major in computer science. Finally! That was what I wanted him to do in the first place. Does this sound familiar to anyone? He was an excellent computer student, straight A's all the way. He received his BS in computer science at Marist College in 1987 and then was awarded a research assistantship at Georgia Tech in Atlanta.

Gary was much more into math and science than David. He majored in engineering and took several computer courses too. He was the only person during his two years at the community college to make A's in general and organic chemistry and physics. He graduated from the community college with a 4.00. We were so proud of both of them. Gary joined David at Georgia Tech in 1989 majored in computer engineering. They both earned their MS degrees there.

David worked one year at the Center of Disease Control in

Atlanta, in their computer center. Near the end of his first year there he was interviewed by a representative of a new group that eventually became known as webmd.com. He was put in charge of designing and implementing software that is used by doctors all over the country. He had 10 other computer people working under him. At the present time David is still doing the same kind of work, but is working for a group called Emdeon.

Gary became an expert in information technology and is working for a pharmaceutical research facility in the research triangle in Morrisville, NC, west of Raleigh. He loves his work.

Vanessa (grandaughter) was born, 2003

My daughter-in-law, Yaxu, is a very special young lady. She was born in Tianjin, China. She lived there with her parents and brother. She attended a Chinese university and majored in engineering. When she finished four years at the university, she was allowed to go to the USA to continue her education. She was an excellent student at the Chinese

120

university. She had to be very good to be allowed to go to the USA for graduate work. It is my understanding that only the upper 10% of those graduating from college in China were permitted to continue in our country.

She attended Oklahoma State and majored in business administration. She had studied English in China. She arrived in the USA late and had already missed some classes. She was an engineering student in China and business administration was a completely new field of study. She was in a different country, speaking a different language, and majoring in a different discipline. She was a super student! Nothing was going to stop this young lady. She earned her Master's degree and interviewed for a job with a company that had an opening in Atlanta.

A former acquaintance of David's knew Yaxu in Oklahoma and asked him to help her when she arrived in Atlanta. He did so and they started dating. He brought her to our home for Christmas in 1999. She did not speak English very well, but understood most of what she heard. We played a lot of monopoly while she was here. That seemed to help her relax. We were all together and we got to know her that way.

David and Yaxu were married in April of 2000. The wedding was wonderful. We met Yaxu's parents at the wedding. They are very nice people. They did not speak English. Her mother came to Atlanta before the birth of her first grandchild, Vanessa, in June, 2003. She stayed at their home for two years and was so much help to them. She does not speak English, but they get along so well. She returned to China when Vanessa was two. Now she and her husband are both in Atlanta, and have been there since Jason, my grandson, was born in March, 2007. They are there to help while Jason is very young. David and Yaxu are so grateful to them for their help. Yaxu is a wonderful wife to my son and mother to our grandchildren. We are so proud of David, Yaxu, Vanessa and Jason. They are a wonderful family!!

Thank goodness that none of my children or grandchildren are diabetic. David is now 42 and Gary is 39. They have beautiful homes and happy lives. Gary is still single.

It was Christmas, 1999 when we first met Yaxu.

David and Yaxu in China, 1999

Wedding, April, 2000

Gary, David and Vanessa, 2003

124

Family, 2007

Jason Is Born, 2007

Vanessa and Jason, 2008

David's family, 2009

126

CHAPTER 16....My Retirement and Double Diabetes

After starting some of the newer insulins in the early 1990s I began gaining weight. By the mid 1990s I had gained more than 40 pounds. Exercising more and eating less did not seem to help at that time. My daily insulin dosage was increasing. In 1998 my insulin dosage had increased 40% and Dr. B. decided that I was experiencing insulin resistance. At that time I was a Type 1 with Type 2 symptoms. That is called "double diabetes".

My performance on campus was not so good in the mid 1990s because of these new developments. Full-time teaching made me feel so tired and my energy was zapped after my morning classes. It was very difficult for me to find the stamina to teach afternoon and evening classes. It was not possible for me to have any enthusiasm when teaching later in the day. The last good year was 1993. After that year everything went steadily downhill. We had planned for my retiring when I was 62 so we would be receiving my social security.

In the 1990s we found that our well was polluted. Several other families had the same problem. Other wells had dried up and drilling was not producing more water. The neighborhood was offered a deal by a private water company. Every family on our street was required to pay equal amounts for hooking up to the new water system. That was an expense we were not expecting. That expense, combined with the cost of our children's college education, was a great burden. We were very heavily in debt. I taught lots of overload and summer school in order to help pay off some of our debts.

Our sons had their MS degrees and good jobs. That was very important to us. My teaching was really getting to me, but then in 1997 something wonderful happened. The county offered retirement incentives to retiring faculty members. We received 70% of my annual salary as an incentive after my retirement in June of that year. That enabled us to pay off all our remaining debts. A miracle just when we needed it. Part-time teaching provided us with extra money until I qualified for social security.

In late 1998 Dr. B. told me there was a new product called Avandia being used in Europe. It was not yet introduced in this country because there was a chance it caused liver damage. By 1999 it was considered safe and I started taking Avandia tablets twice per day. In just a few days I needed less insulin and after a few weeks, my dosages returned to normal. My energy had returned and my mood, and outlook on life, were much improved.

Part-time teaching was good for me and I almost wanted to become full-time again, but that was impossible. My full-time position had been filled. Being full-time again would have required giving up both social security and retirement income. Retirement was wonderful and my good health had been restored. Being overweight was my only big problem at that time.

In 1999 I started using a 75/25 Humalog mix in an insulin pen. That resulted in lower blood sugar and A1c's, but it also caused me to have many highs and lows. After a few years I asked Dr. B. to let me start using vials of Humalog separately from the mix when carb counting required more bolus than my mix was giving me. I also needed the extra Humalog for correcting my highs. He hesitated letting me use the vials of Humalog because he knew I had hypos rather frequently. He eventually agreed to let me do that and I was finally using a basal/bolus method of control for the first time.

Using carb counting and determining my Humalog dosages by knowing the number of carbs in my meals and snacks gave me much better control. The number of hypos was much less with this kind of control. Anita never again had to have paramedics visit our home. There were still some hypos, but Anita's help was rarely needed. When they were too low for me to handle Anita was able to feed me glucose tablets and test my blood sugar repeatedly, until I improved enough that I could take over. My hypos were not nearly as bad or as frequent as they were before using basal/bolus control.

After retiring and teaching part time for a few years I was having good blood sugar control with A1c's below 6.0. Doctor B. would walk into his office with a big smile on his face and tell me my A1c was a nondiabetic number. He would go over every line of my extensive lab report and discuss anything that needed discussing. He had much blood work done every three months. Almost everything in the lab reports was good except for a few occasions. My cholesterol was 280+ on one visit. Dr. B. prescribed several medicines and Zocor worked best, with no side effects. In November, 2007, my cholesterol had dropped to 128. I had bad reactions to Mevacor and Questran but Zocor has been very good for me.

In the 1990s my kidneys showed some sign of hyper filtration. Altace, a medicine primarily intended for lowering blood pressure, was prescribed. Altace has a side effect of stabilizing hyper filtration in the kidneys. My kidneys have been great ever since. In early 2007 my blood pressure was 145. The Altace was then helping both my kidneys and my blood pressure, but it was not enough. Instead of increasing my Altace dosage Dr. B. gave me a prescription for water pills.

My blood pressure has been good ever since. I test my

blood pressure at home too and it is always between 115 and 135. Dr. B. is the only doctor I have had who did extensive testing like this. After these issues were resolved my blood tests were consistently good for several years, until 2002.

In August of 2002 my PSA count was 4.2. The previous year it was 3.0. This test determines the size of the prostate gland. Now 4.2 is a very low number and would not normally be anything to cause concern. Dr. B., however, is very cautious on all matters. He sent me to a urologist who told me he wanted to do a biopsy, just in case. His concern was not the number itself, it was that 4.2 was a 40% increase over the 3.0 from the preceding year. A 40% increase is significant. The biopsy showed I had cancer. After an MRI and other tests were performed it was determined that the cancer was totally contained in the gland. The cancerous tumors were so small that they did not show up on the X-ray. They were microscopic in size.

Dr. B's cautious nature resulted in such an early diagnosis that I did not have to have surgery to remove the gland. That is considered to be major surgery when it is done. Radiation treatment began in January and concluded in early March of 2003. On each of 41 visits to radiology I received 6 jolts of high intensity X-rays into my lower abdomen to destroy the cancerous cells. That is a lot of radiation. It worked perfectly, but there were very unpleasant side effects that continued for over two years.

I developed anemia that lasted almost one year. Iron tablets took care of that problem. Damage was done to my intestines but it was kept under control. When the bleeding in my bowels stopped two years later I was in good shape. The radiologist said there was an 80% chance that the cancer would never return. To date it has not. Males used to be checked for prostate cancer in their early 60s. In present

130

times men should be checked by the time they are 40 because prostate cancer has been found in men who are in their 40s.

My 57 pounds of overweight was still bothering me in the early 2000s. I bought a tread mill, and started strengthening my leg muscles. After several months I could walk a mile in 20 minutes, using a 7.0 incline on the machine. By reducing my daily carb intake to 150 carbs and using the treadmill, I managed to lose 26 pounds. There was still 31 pounds of overweight, but I felt great and my waist size was 4 inches smaller. Buying new trousers felt good. Stabilizing and not gaining more weight was very comforting.

I taught at a NY state community college and my pension is paid by NY state. My secondary health insurance plan is the NY State Empire Plan. Medicare is my primary health insurance, but there are so many things that it does not cover. Medicare would not cover my pump and some of the supplies and it does not cover my prescribed medicines. It helps in the reduction of prices of doctor's office visits and hospital visits. Empire covers the pump, most of the supplies, the medicines and, in short, everything that Medicare does not cover.

School teachers may not have great salaries, but the fringe benefits here in NY state are great. There is one big down side to using the Empire Plan. We must visit doctors, hospitals and labs that are participating in order to get the maximum benefit of the Empire plan. Outside of NY it is much harder to find participating members. For that reason we have decided to stay in NY.

Our children and grandchildren live in Georgia and North Carolina. We fly to Atlanta at least once each year to see David, Yaxu, Vanessa and Jason. Gary drives from Raleigh to Atlanta to be with us. It is expensive for us to fly and getting through the airports is hard on us. It would take almost 20 hours on the road to drive to Atlanta. We do not know how much longer we can make the flights. Our grandchildren are going to grow up and we will have seen them so infrequently while they were still children. We see them on Webcam, but that is a very poor replacement for being there.

So whose idea was it to send my sons to Georgia Tech for graduate work? IT WAS MY IDEA! DUH!!! They loved the south and stayed there. They have wonderful jobs and we are so proud of them but we do not get to see them very often. I feel like an idiot! I could have had David and Gary apply to northern colleges. The southern colleges are much less expensive. The state colleges there are much cheaper too. Georgia Tech is highly ranked in computer education, so that is where we sent them. That made it much easier to afford their educational expenses. I am afraid we will not have a very close relationship with our grand kids when they are grown. This is my biggest regret in my present day life.

Carpentry is a one of my hobbies

CHAPTER 17 .... My Diabetes Complications

The house we bought in Kingston, NY, was very much in need of repair. It was a fixer-upper and we got it cheap, but the mortgage payments were still very hard to make. There was an old mail box on the edge of our front lawn mounted on a thick cedar post. While trying to pull it out of the ground I heard a popping sound, and felt a sharp pain in my chest. The pain did not last long and I got a shovel and dug around the post. There was about three feet of it beneath the ground's surface. The ground was soft, but I should not have done all that pulling. The pain grew worse later on so Anita drove me to the ER and my heart was thoroughly checked.

They saw nothing wrong with my heart and they could not diagnose the problem. My chest hurt for weeks. The pain is still there when I engage in any activity that stretches my chest muscles. There was probably a muscle that was partially torn by that heavy pulling. I cannot carry more than 50 pounds, lift heavy weights, or even hug my wife very hard without hurting that muscle.

In my late 40's I began having pain in my arms and hands. A neurologist had me report to the hospital for an EMG test. No one locally performed an EMG back then. Someone from the Albany Medical Center, 50 miles away, came to Kingston one day per week to give EMG's at the hospital. The EMG did not show any sign of carpal tunnel, even though the doctor thought that was my problem. My neurologist prescribed a body scan which required a shot of radioactive fluid. The scan showed arthritis in my arms, legs, back and neck. An arthritis specialist told me that my arthritis was probably due to my diabetes. Diabetics are more likely that non diabetics to have arthritis.

The only thing that really concerned me at that time was the very annoying pain in my hands and lower arms. A couple of years passed and I went to a second neurologist. The results were the same. The same fellow from Albany gave me the EMG and again found no carpal tunnel problem. About five years later the pain was more intense and I saw a third neurologist. That time a member of their staff gave me the EMG. She diagnosed carpal tunnel and ulnar nerve problems and told me the damage was extensive. She said that it must have been present at the time the other EMG's had been given.

The fellow from Albany had not properly administered the test, or his equipment was defective. A neurosurgeon performed carpal tunnel surgery on my right wrist. Another neurosurgeon performed ulnar nerve transposition surgery on the same arm the following year. The surgeons told me that the nerve damage was so advanced, that the surgeries would keep the damage from getting any worse, but they would not reverse the damage already done. They were right. Pain has continued during the ensuing years, but it has not become significantly worse.

I asked the surgeons if the nerve damage in my arms could possibly be due to diabetes. They said it was possible, but there was no way of knowing. Many things can cause carpal tunnel problems and other nerve damage. All that carpentry work could have caused it. Diabetics are more prone to have nerve damage.

Cataracts were removed from both of my eyes when I was in my late 50's. My ophthamologist also diagnosed some retinopathy, but it did not require laser treatment. The retinopathy showed up in little patches, but disappeared in a few weeks. I have breaks in some of the blood vessels in my right eye at the present time. My eye doctor says that it may be due to my diabetes, but is not retinopathy. It cannot be treated by laser surgery because of its location. It will require conventional surgery. The doctor said I could wait until it gives me more of a problem with my eyesight. It is like looking through a wet pane of glass, but it only bothers me when I am reading or doing close work. It is now getting worse so I may have surgery done later this year. These problems may be due to diabetes. Both cataracts and nerve damage are more common among diabetics.

I was diagnosed with gout in May of 2007. The medicine prescribed for inflammation, or the inflammation itself, caused me to have very high blood sugar for several days. Allopurinol was prescribed for my gout. Those tablets reduced the level of uric acid in my joints. My blood sugar returned to normal and the gout pain was gone. Excessive uric acid in the joints is what causes gout. My first gout attack appeared in the base joint of my big toe and, eight months later, the second attack appeared in the heel of my right foot. My third gout attack occurred in October, 2009, but Allopurinol took care of the problem again. Gout is also more common among diabetics.

In my 60's I developed neuropathy in my left foot and ankles. There was also nerve damage in my ears. The neuropathy was quite bad and it kept me up at night until my blood sugar control improved. Pumping insulin tightened my control even more and there is rarely any neuropathy pain now. An audiologist diagnosed nerve damage in both of my ears. That has resulted in partial hearing loss. I have a lot of difficulty hearing high frequency sounds, unless they are very loud. I bought hearing aids and wore them for eight months, but they did not help. Some people have to speak louder in order for me to hear them properly.

All the problems mentioned here, except for the muscle damage in my chest, may possibly be linked to my diabetes. None of them, however, are all that bad. There are very few things that I can no longer do, but there are limitations. My arms may be somewhat weak, but my legs are strong, with a lot of muscle. I could walk 3 miles in one hour on roads with a lot of hills in 2008. That is my favorite exercise. In 2009 I had to be satisfied with 2.5 miles in one hour. My pace is somewhat slower now.

In the spring and summer of 2009 I put new wood on the back of my house and caulked and painted it. This year I aim to do the same kind of work on the north side. The whole house will have been resided by the end of this year. It is very comforting to me that I am still able to do this kind work at my age, after 64 years of diabetes.

So I have experienced arthritis, carpal tunnel and ulnar nerve damage, cataracts, mild retinopathy, neuropathy, broken blood vessels in one eye, nerve damage in my ears, and gout. All of those problems occurred after 40 years of diabetes. Prior to that time there were no complications whatsoever.

All of my complications have been minor. Good health after all my high blood sugar during my early years is a blessing. There are very many non diabetics who have health problems much worse than mine. My working so hard to have good diabetes control has helped to keep me in very good physical condition. My diabetes may very well be partially responsible for my good health. Some people tell me that it is due to my having good genes. Maybe that is part of the explanation, but all my hard work has undoubtedly played a major role in keeping me very healthy.

Research has shown that diabetics with good A1c's might still have complications if they have a roller coaster type of control. A diabetic with many highs and lows can still have a good blood sugar average and A1c, but the rise and fall of the blood sugar levels can cause complications in the long run.

There is a term called "standard deviation" (SD) which measures the amount of rise and fall above and below an individual's average blood sugar level. A person with many highs and lows that differ greatly from their blood sugar average will have a large SD. A person with moderate highs and lows that differ much less from the blood sugar average will have a smaller SD. Ideal blood sugar control would require a good blood sugar average and A1c, accompanied by a low SD. The ADA (American Diabetes Assoc.) states that a SD less than 30 is desirable. I do not consider an SD that high to be desirable. My SD is usually between 20 and 25, but I would like it to be less than 20.

CHAPTER 18....Pumping Insulin

In 2002 I was in good shape physically and mentally. My A1c was less than 6.0 and my blood sugar control was good, but I wanted better. Part time teaching was fun and flying twice each year to Atlanta to see my sons, daughter-in-law and grandchildren was something Anita and I enjoyed very much. My exercising continued after radiation treatment for prostate cancer. My lower carb diet, carb counting and the logging of my diet and control all helped me very much.

In late 2004 I felt great. Cutting down on my daily carb intake and exercising rigorously on my treadmill or walking outdoors enabled me to lose 26 pounds. My A1c's remained below 6.0. My last part-time class at the college was in 2004. Retirement made me feel like a fish out of water. The part-time teaching had helped, but when it stopped my life was rather boring much of the time.

Carpentry and working on my house is one of my favorite hobbies. Painting the whole house inside and out, replacing the interior doors, remodeling the master bedroom, and building a home entertainment center in my oldest son's former bedroom kept me occupied. That is where I sit to type these chapters. By 2006 there was much less construction work to be done and my life was boring again.

I started posting on the dLife diabetes website. Janis Roszler, a moderator there, is a CDE and an RD and she teaches people all about pumping. My control with injections was quite good, but she recommended pumping insulin because of the many freedoms it offers. Several friends on dLife started encouraging me as well. The idea of only one needle every three days, instead of 6-8 daily injections with my basal/bolus routine, was very appealing. The freedom and convenience that a pump would provide made pumping seem very attractive.

On the day of my next appointment with Dr. B. I asked him about using a pump. He said it was not a good idea even though he had recommended pumping a few years earlier when my control was not as good. He thought it was unnecessary since my control had improved so much. He told me that several of his diabetic patients had worse control after starting to pump and they had more hypos as well. He would not support my pumping. Dr. B. is a specialist in internal medicine and has always been there for me for all my problems. I decided to get a second opinion about pumping.

We found an endocrinologist in Poughkeepsie and made an appointment for Jan. 30, 2007. That was about the time that I was posting less on dLife and joined Diabetes Daily (DD). My new friends there encouraged me to pump and get still better control. The endo approved of my pumping and sent me to get some blood tests required by Medicare. Something about the lab results did not meet with the approval of Medicare and they would not finance my pump. That was very disappointing and it seemed that pumping was out of the picture. The pump itself would cost me more than $6,000 and the monthly supplies were also too expensive for my budget.

The endo's office phoned me the following week and told me that my secondary insurance would cover the cost of the pump and all of the supplies. I was thrilled! The NY State Empire Plan is my secondary health insurance plan. All employees of the state are eligible to have that insurance. While teaching full time the college paid my premiums and the coverage was for my whole family. After retirement the college pays half of our premiums for as long as I live and we pay the other half. It is a great insurance plan.

The lady from the endo's office asked me to pick a color for my pump and the order was sent out. Anita and I went to the diabetes education center at a hospital in Poughkeepsie and met my trainer and a dietitian. They gave me a kit containing a manual and a CD and told me to become thoroughly familiar with the Minimed 522 pump, before the pump they had ordered arrived at my home. I had also ordered the book "Pumping Insulin" by John Walsh. It was highly recommended by my friends on the DD website. My friends on DD and on Janis Roszler's site were all cheering me on.

The pump arrived in late April and that gave me one week to have a hands-on experience with it. I wore it 24/7 and became accustomed to the feel of it. Pump training started in early May. It went smoothly, but my trainer wanted to take it very slowly. We liked her very much, but four different trips for training was not necessary. It is probably a standard procedure applied to all her patients. We made a separate trip to talk with the dietitian about carb counting. My charts convinced her that I understood carb counting and was ready to start pumping. Cooperating with my endo was necessary since she insisted on all this training. Her office was in the same building as the diabetes education center. They all work together.

In the last week of May I was pumping saline solution, just for practice. That solution put too much salt into my body and there was a lot of water retention. The water pills I had been taking for water retention were not enough. My trainer said to stop pumping saline. June 19 was my starting date with my pump. The endo looked at my charts and told my trainer the numbers to put into my pump. My basal rates, carb ratios, targets, insulin sensitivity factor and all the rest. I went home full of enthusiasm and was really looking forward to the next few days.

Later that day my blood sugar was over 200 and climbing. My endo did not want me to change anything without her approval. I called her that evening at her home. She had given me several phone numbers. She did not seem to know what to tell me. She had me change a couple of things but it did not help. That was when I decided to take charge of my own control. Before doing so, I disconnected the pump and resumed injections for a few days until good control was reestablished. My math and statistical background and 61 years of injections enabled me to do this by myself.

All the numbers in my program had to be changed. After a few days things were going much better, but there was trouble with the needles in my Quick sets. They kept pulling out of my body. Putting my clothes on and off, rolling over in bed and other such things seemed to cause this problem. Very high blood sugar occurred whenever this happened. Testing for ketones was necessary every time my test was 250 or higher. Injections enabled me to get good control before re-attaching the pump.

My friends on DD told me about the Sure-T infusion set. It is made very differently and the needle is very unlikely to pull out of my body once it is taped securely. I ordered a supply of the Sure-T's and have been using them ever since. They are great! My control was much improved and my analysis of my testing from mid-July to late August showed control equal to what I had before pumping. My lab visit in the third week of August was only 10 weeks after my pumping began. I expected the A1c to be very high because of all the high blood sugar during the beginning stages of pumping. My A1c was 5.6 before pumping. When I went to Dr. B's office in late August my A1c was 5.7. That was so surprising!

The A1c test covered the three month period preceding the

lab date. My control was rather poor with very high numbers during the last 11 days of June and the first 10 days of July, but things were quite good for the rest of July and all of August. The numbers for the first month of the three month period covered by the A1c are not so influential in the A1c result. The numbers during the second month have a greater influence, but it is the numbers during the third month that have by far the greatest influence on the A1c result. My numbers were very good for the last 6 weeks of the period covered by my A1c test and that overshadowed the bad numbers preceding that six week period. That is why my A1c was so good.

My success with pumping at that time made me very happy. Being able to sleep late in the mornings was great. Delaying meals, varying my eating schedule, and eating very different types of meals no longer affected my blood sugar. Those are only a few of the freedoms offered by pumping. Doing those things while injecting my insulin would have caused problems. Counting the carbs ever so carefully and pumping the insulin that my pump indicated to be the correct amount was working very well. The very rigid schedule that was so important while still on injections was no longer necessary. I was unchained and free to live like a more normal person. The machine attached to me worked very much like a pancreas and I was very pleased with my pumping experience.

CHAPTER 19....Pumping Problems and Other Disappointments

Pumping was wonderful, but there were problems encountered later on that were very annoying. These problems were not due to pumping. They were problems that would have occurred even if I was not pumping. Every time the seasons change the temperatures fluctuate, and so do my blood sugar levels. Having to deal with this in October and November was difficult. There were many highs and lows and my control was not as good as it had been in August and September. Much of my programming had to be altered until the colder weather of late November, when the temperatures were more stable. I tend to need more insulin in colder weather and less in warmer weather. Many diabetics have told me they have this problem, but apparently there are some who don't.

Diabetics who live in parts of the country where the temperatures are more stable the whole year may not have that problem. Diabetics in the deep south may not notice much difference in insulin dosages throughout the year. A friend in southern California told me that his dosages remain very constant, but the temperatures there are very stable. The temperatures here in NY can vary as much as 20 degrees Fahrenheit in a week's time.

In December there were some "no delivery" alarms on my pump. After changing my infusion set the alarms were still there. The help on the Minimed hot line is very good. A very young-sounding lady talked to me for about 20 minutes. She had me give her a lot of information from my pump's memory and she decided the pump was not at fault. Then she asked what part of my body I was using for my infusion set placement. My upper abdomen had been used for most of my injections for 61 years and my infusion sets were placed there too. I occasionally used my legs when injecting, but it was my upper abdomen for many, many years.

The young lady told me to start using other suitable body parts and let my upper abdomen rest. She thought I had scar tissue due to overuse of that part of my body. She was right! Using my lower abdomen below the belt line made the absorption of my insulin much faster and more stable. There were no more alarms. It was amazing that a young lady who sounded like she might be in her early twenties could solve my problem so quickly. My endo did not know the cause of my problem.

There were still problems. The absorption was so fast that the programming on my pump had to be changed again to combat the low blood sugar. There were some lows in the 30-60 range for several weeks until I adjusted to the new absorption rates. This resulted in my using less insulin. It was not until February of 2008 that everything was under control. That month was the best since I had started pumping. My average blood sugar for that month was 88 and my standard deviation was 27. An average of 88 is not low for me since my target is 90. That is a bigger standard deviation than I wanted. Something less than 20 is my goal. I rarely have a high above 140 now. The discovery of my scar tissue has helped me very much.

Many of the big jumps from high to low blood sugar, for perhaps forty or more years prior to pumping, may have been due to uneven absorption and scar tissue. No doctor ever told me to rotate my sites and use different body parts to prevent scar tissue from forming. I remember very clearly that there were many times it was difficult to insert the needles into my upper abdomen. The skin was tough from scar tissue, I am convinced of that. There were times when my injections hit soft tissue and other times when it was hard. That phone call to Minimed resulted in my very first exposure to scar tissue being a problem for diabetics.

Why didn't my doctors ever tell me to rotate my sites? Did they assume I knew? Many diabetics have lots of ups and downs in their blood sugar levels and many of them for unexplainable reasons. In some cases this may be due to scar tissue developing because of using the same region on their bodies for an extended period of time. Rotation of sites on a regular basis will prevent this from happening. Absorption will be complete and more even. Very high blood sugar can occur when insulin is trapped in an area affected by scar tissue. Under these conditions the insulin reaches the blood stream much too slowly.

There have been many things that my doctors should have known, but did not tell me during my 64 years as a diabetic. In chapter 13 it was mentioned that a low carb diet was used to help diabetics, even before insulin was discovered. It was known in the early 1920's that a low carb diet was helpful to diabetics. Even as early as the 1600's there were doctors who thought that reducing the number of carbs in a diabetic's diet would help reduce the amount of sugar in the blood. So why didn't my doctor in 1945, the year of my diagnosis, tell my parents to limit the number of carbs in my diet? Why did he tell them to not give me sugar, but fail to mention carbs?

None of my four doctors during my first 35 or so years as a diabetic ever mentioned this to me. My first exposure to carb counting occurred in the 1980's while I was reading a magazine article about diabetes in the waiting room at my eye doctor's office. Perhaps some of my previous doctors assumed that I already knew about carbs and rotation of sites.

It would be great if every doctor who has diabetic patients

would hand them a pamphlet containing important facts about the proper care and treatment of diabetes. All diabetic patients should receive this pamphlet even if they have been diabetic for many years. If I had known these things during my early years, much of my high blood sugar could have been avoided.

Fortunately, I have not developed serious complications, but what about all the diabetics who did develop terrible problems with their eyes and kidneys in their earlier years? How about the ones who had heart attacks, strokes and amputations because they did not know they were supposed to follow a low carb diet? This discussion is sounding like a rant, but it is something that has bothered me very much since the 1980s when I discovered that counting carbs is so important. My insulin dosages are now determined by my knowing the number of grams of carbohydrates in my meals and snacks. This is the very best form of control and my pump makes it very easy to do.

CHAPTER 20.... Type 1 Diabetes, Causes, Statistics and Discussion

What causes Type 1 diabetes? There are many answers to that question. The cause is not always genetically based. There are many other possible causes. It is also interesting to study the statistics associated with all types of diabetes. Just how many of us are there in the USA? Another topic of great interest to me is the likelihood that Type 1 diabetics may pass on their diabetes to their children. These and related topics are discussed in this chapter.

The blood glucose level in people who are healthy is regulated by insulin and other hormones. The pancreas produces insulin and it also produces other enzymes that help to digest food. When there is insufficient insulin produced by the islet cells in the pancreas the blood glucose rises to abnormally high levels. This causes hyperglycemia and the other commonly seen symptoms of poorly controlled Type 1 diabetes.

There are two forms of Type 1 diabetes. They are called idiopathic Type 1 and immune-mediated Type 1. Idiopathic Type 1 is a rare form with no known cause. Immune-mediated Type 1 is the one that is most commonly seen. The remaining information in this chapter refers to this form of Type 1 diabetes.

Approximately 10% of the diabetics in the United States have Type 1 diabetes. It is estimated that there are about 24 million diabetics (diagnosed and undiagnosed combined) in the United States at the present time, so the number of Type 1 diabetics is approximately 2,400,000. The likelihood of Type 1 diabetes is greater than that of almost all other severe chronic diseases of childhood.

Type 1 diabetes is usually diagnosed in children or

adolescents. It used to be called juvenile diabetes, or insulin dependent diabetes mellitus. My doctor called it "sugar diabetes" during my childhood. Now we know that Type 1 diabetes also occurs in older people. I have read of people in their 80's being diagnosed with Type 1, so it can obviously occur at any age.

Family members of a Type 1 diabetic are less likely to have diabetes than the family members of a Type 2. None of my family members or relatives have ever been diagnosed with Type 1 diabetes. I have had several relatives with Type 2 diabetes, but none with Type 1. There was a large study of families with Type 1 diabetes. The study revealed that less than 4% of parents and 6% of siblings of a person with Type 1 diabetes also had Type 1 diabetes. Children of a Type 1 diabetic father are more likely to become Type 1 than children of a Type 1 diabetic mother.

Diabetic parents are always concerned about the genetic transmission of Type 1 diabetes, the odds for Type 1 being passed on to a child.

According to the Islets Of Hope website, the children of a Type 1 father have a 6% chance of becoming Type 1. It is also noted that if either parent was diagnosed before they were 11 years old, the risk is doubled. Since I was diagnosed when I was 6, my sons have an approximately 12% chance of becoming Type 1. The ages of my sons are 39 and 42 and they do not have diabetes at this time. The odds that they will never be Type 1 are definitely in their favor.

If a Type 1 mother has a child before she is 25 years old then there is a 4% risk that her child will become Type 1. If a Type 1 mother has a child when she is 25 or older there is only a 1% risk that her child will become Type 1.

If both parents are Type 1 their children have a 50% chance of becoming Type 1.

A child that has a parent or sibling with Type 1 diabetes has a 2 to 6% risk of developing the disease. The risk is higher if both a parent and sibling have Type 1 diabetes.

It is important to note that 80% of people with Type 1 diabetes do not have another relative with Type 1 diabetes. It is also important to realize that many people have the genetic predisposition for Type 1 diabetes, but never get the disease.

Research has shown that breastfeeding a baby at least three months decreases the risk of Type 1 diabetes.

Causes of Type 1 Diabetes

Autoimmune disorders are very commonly seen in the development of Type 1 diabetes. This occurs when the body's immune system is faulty and sees one of its own tissues as being foreign. If the islet cells in the pancreas are attacked and destroyed, there is no insulin produced and Type 1 diabetes results.

The reason for the development of autoimmune Type 1 diabetes is unknown, but it is usually due to a genetic tendency. Sometimes it follows a viral infection. Some people are more genetically prone to develop this autoimmune disorder due to progressive failure of the insulin-producing beta cells in the pancreas. It can also occur when the pancreas is destroyed by disease, alcohol, toxins, trauma or surgical removal.

Other underlying causes or triggers that could cause Type 1 diabetes include Hemochromatosis (a hereditary disease involving the presence of excessive iron in body tissues and organs, including the pancreas); Polyendochrine syndromes (syndromes that cause autoimmune diseases in various body glands); Cystic fibrosis; Addison's disease and Pancreatitis.

There are conditions for which Type 1 diabetes is sometimes a symptom. Those conditions may also be potential causes of Type 1 diabetes. They include Dorsal pancreas agenesis and pancreatic beta cell agenesis (the failure of an organ to develop during embryonic growth); Mental retardation; Dysmorphism (a malformation in the anatomy); Hypogonadism (when the sex glands produce little or no hormones); Pyogenic or infectious arthritis (bacterial infection in the joints, which can occur in any age group) and Pyoderma gangrenosum (a skin ulceration which sometimes also affects other organs).

Various viruses have been mentioned as potential triggers of Type 1 diabetes. They include Congenital rubella, Coxsackie B virus, Cytomegalovirus (CMV), Enteroviruses, Adenovirus, Mumps virus and Epstein-Barr virus.

Medicines that can trigger Type 1

Some medicines are associated with elevated blood glucose levels and can cause diabetes control to become much more difficult. In some cases these medicines can cause the onset of diabetes. Many of these medicines, however, are not commonly used. A few medicines that are widely used and are firmly associated with elevated blood glucose include glucocorticoids, thiazide diuretics and beta-blockers. Glucocorticoids stimulate the production of glucose. The glucocorticoids include prednisone, dexamethasone, and triamcinolone. These drugs have a significant effect on the metabolism of carbohydrates and can be used to reduce severe inflammation. Rheumatoid arthritis, severe asthma,

154

and inflammatory bowel disease are among the conditions for which these medications may be used.

Antipsychotic drugs, and in particular, olanzapine and clozapine, can elevate blood glucose, cause weight gain, and increase blood lipids. These drugs also raise the risk for diabetic ketoacidosis.

Acute asthma and arthritis are the diseases that two of my friends have and Prednisone gave them great relief but diabetes resulted from long-term use of the medication. A great majority of people using these medications do not become diabetics. There is only a small percentage of these people who do become diabetics.

A link that discusses causes of Type 1:

http://www.wrongdiagnosis.com/d/diab1/causes.htm

Type 1 Diabetes Trialnet

Type 1 Diabetes TrialNet is an international network of researchers who are exploring ways to prevent, delay and reverse the progression of Type 1 diabetes.

TrialNet mainly conducts two types of studies:
Studies for people who do not have Type 1 diabetes, but are at increased risk because they have a family member with the disease and Studies for those recently diagnosed with Type 1 diabetes (within 100 days). There are many different studies being made by TrialNet. The one that interests me most is the study that involves taking a blood sample from the children or siblings of a Type 1 and determining if the gene that could cause Type 1 is present. I have read about someone in Atlanta having his children tested by TrialNet for this reason. He is awaiting the results of those tests. I can imagine how happy he would be if the

gene is not present in his children. If the gene is present then he will at least be able take precautionary steps to test them with a glucometer and watch their diets.

My son, David, also lives in Atlanta. I have told him about TrialNet so that he may consider having my grand children tested. If TrialNet had existed when my children were living at home I would have had them examined to see if they possessed the gene that indicated a predisposition of having Type 1 during their lifetimes.

Some Startling Statistics

According to the National Institutes of Health the Prevalence of Diagnosed and Undiagnosed Diabetes in the United States, All Ages, 2007:

Total: 23.6 million people—7.8 percent of the population—have diabetes.

Diagnosed: 17.9 million people

Undiagnosed: 5.7 million people (an estimate)

It is estimated that 850,000 to 1.7 million Americans have Type 1 diabetes. Of those, about 125,000 are kids 19 and under. It was reported that an additional 30,000 Americans develop Type 1 diabetes every year, 13,000 of whom are children. A more updated report indicates there are more than 2 million Type 1 diabetics at the present time. That suggests that the rate of increase has accelerated.

Prevalence of Diagnosed and Undiagnosed Diabetes among People Aged 20 Years or Older, United States, 2007:

Age 20 years or older: 23.5 million, or 10.7 percent, of all people in this age group have diabetes.

Age 60 years or older: 12.2 million, or 23.1 percent, of all people in this age group have diabetes.

Men: 12.0 million, or 11.2 percent, of all men aged 20 years or older have diabetes.

Women: 11.5 million, or 10.2 percent, of all women aged 20 years or older have diabetes.

Non-Hispanic whites: 14.9 million, or 9.8 percent, of all non-Hispanic whites aged 20 years or older have diabetes.

Non-Hispanic blacks: 3.7 million, or 14.7 percent, of all non-Hispanic blacks aged 20 years or older have diabetes.

For the year 2006 diabetes was the seventh leading cause of death in the United States. It has also been found that diabetes is likely to be under reported as a cause of death.

A discussion among Type 1 diabetics in an online support group.

On the tudiabetes.com website a very interesting discussion took place in 2008. The title of the discussion was "What Causes Type I Diabetes? State Your Theory". It was a very popular topic and there were seven pages of replies. The following list is based on those replies. The people involved are Type 1 diabetics and members of the support group on tudiabetes.com. In most instances these are the opinions of the diabetics themselves. I enjoyed this discussion.

Many members said their Type 1 was triggered by a virus and that viruses caused the damage that resulted in their diabetes. The viruses mentioned included scarlet fever, bronchitis, strep throat, asthma, bladder infection, lung infection, chicken pox and mumps. I mentioned in my first chapter that I had mumps and chicken pox during the months preceding my diagnosis.

There were several members who pointed out that Type 1 is often hereditary, so the predisposition to their diabetes was genetic. There were also many members who stated that they had no relatives with Type 1. That is also true among my own relatives. There is no Type 1 among my wife's relatives either.

Alcoholism caused one of the members to have terrible damage to his pancreas. His pancreas and parts of other internal organs had to be surgically removed.

Another member said that diabetes can be slowly developing in a person's system for as much as seven years prior to diagnosis. That member said that when there is about 10% of the insulin producing cells remaining, the symptoms of Type 1 diabetes begin to appear.

A few members said that Graves disease and diseases of the thyroid gland had caused their Type 1.

Other factors that some members feel triggered their Type 1 included stress, a deficiency in vitamin D, prescription drugs, major invasive surgery, and trauma. Environmental factors like mold and toxins were also mentioned as possible triggers.

Dr. J. Bart Classen, an immunologist in Maryland, says vaccines given to young children can lead to Type 1. Vaccines for mumps, measles, chicken pox, and other diseases are frequently given to children within a short period of time. Dr Classen says that the Type 1 in as many as 80% of his young diabetic patients were due to these vaccines.

Medications that can trigger or even cause Type 1 were discussed. Steroids such as Prednisone were mentioned. I have read about several people whose diabetes resulted from Prednisone. They were taking the medication for other problems and things got out of hand.

CHAPTER 21....Long Lives With Type 1 Diabetes

Many people who know me are of the opinion that I have broken a record and they have not heard of anyone having diabetes so long, and having no serious complications. There are many diabetics who have had diabetes much longer than me. See their stories below.

Bob and Gerald Cleveland, combined, have experienced 154 years of Type 1 diabetes. Bob was 5 when he was diagnosed in 1925. Insulin was first sold just two years earlier. Bob's brother Gerald Cleveland was diagnosed with Type 1 when he was 16. Gerald said that at first it was depressing to know that he had to live with diabetes. He eventually discovered that he was healthier than most people in general. Bob is a retired accountant. Gerald was a teacher, and later a superintendent of schools.

Both brothers say their longevity is due to the healthy lifestyle required to control their diabetes. They give credit to their mother for her care and dedication to their diabetes management.

Gerald Cleveland urges others with diabetes to "pay attention to their health" and to not take chances.

"You can have a pretty liberal life today, as long as you follow certain basic regimens," he says. "Don't forget you're under a certain set of rules, and that if you violate them, you're going to have problems."

Bob, at 90, says he is lucky to be alive and that he is better off than 90 percent of the people where he lives in a retirement community. He says others should listen to their doctors and follow a good food and exercise regimen.

Gladys C. Lester Dull was diagnosed with Type 1 in 1924 when she was 6 years old. Her mother attended educational classes at the Mayo Clinic where Gladys was diagnosed. She learned to weigh the food for her daughter. Her mother weighed everything her daughter ate after that. Gladys had two older and two younger siblings, none of whom were diabetics. All of those siblings have died. Gladys has outlived all of them. She had a sister who died of Alzheimer's disease. Gladys has no signs of Alzheimer's even though the risk is possibly higher among diabetics. "After seeing what my sister went through, I would much rather be a diabetic than have Alzheimer's," Gladys says.

This 91 year old says her longevity comes from being active most of her life, and sticking to her diet. "I give my mother credit for that," she says. Her mother was strict with her, and she is thankful for that. "I have never missed a shot in all these years. To date, I've had over 60,000 of them."

In the summer of 2008 a diabetic friend notified me that the ADA (American Diabetes Association) was looking for diabetics who had lived with diabetes for more than sixty years. The year 2008 was the 60'th anniversary of the *Diabetes Forecast*, the monthly magazine published by the ADA. After joining the ADA site and posting some of my background, one of the people from the magazine staff sent me an email. They were interested in my online story and they wanted to include me in their October issue that year.

On August 1 a professional photographer arrived at my home. His name was John, a young personable fellow. John spent about two hours and snapped many, many pictures. When he arrived I was wearing walking shorts and short sleeves. John asked me to change into different clothes since the magazine's 60'th anniversary edition would be published in October. My wardrobe was not very Octoberish. He wanted me to dress in long pants and long

162

sleeves and he wanted me to do some work in my "workshop". An ADA staff member had read that I had done a lot of carpentry work on my house through the years so they thought it would be neat if they photographed me working with my carpentry tools in my workshop.

My garage is my "workshop" and my tools are very simple but John was not discouraged. I put on some old clothes speckled with paint and John thought that was perfect. He put some bright colored paint cans behind me on a shelf and I started sawing away on a piece of trim in my miter box. About twenty pictures later I picked my Dremel tool and held it to the trim for the next sequence of pictures. It was a hot sultry day and we were sweating, but John was happy. I looked very Octoberish.

We were talking to John about all the rain we had been having and how we had two sump pumps going to remove the water from our basement. When we returned to picture taking I asked John to be sure to get some pictures of the sump pump I was wearing. HA! I meant to say insulin pump. We all got a big laugh out of that! Anita gave me a funny look, she may have wondered if I was having a hypo. HA!

We then went to the back yard for the last set. There are very pretty flowers and gardens that my wife has carefully prepared through the years in our back yard, but John said that did not look appropriate for October. He told me to put my shorts and short sleeved shirt back on. He was down on the ground shooting from an angle that would not show my bare legs. The side of the house and an evergreen were in the background so the summer scenery would not appear in the pictures.

The Octoberish thing was beginning to get to me. John wanted me to smile in every shot so I continued to grin and tried to look happy in the pictures he took. Actually we enjoyed John's visit. He was a very nice fellow. He never took any pictures of Anita, she is very attractive. She was happy about that.

After John left I went back into my house, poured a glass of iced lemonade, turned on a fan, and relaxed in my easy chair. The following week we were notified by the photography department of the magazine that the pictures had turned out great and they wanted me to send them some childhood pictures. I sent a few including one that was taken during the year of my diagnosis in 1945. They used only two of the dozens of pictures that John took, but we were told that that is typical in a situation like that.

When the October issue was released we bought copies and sent them to my sons and my sister. Several diabetic friends in the diabetesdaily.com diabetes support group bought copies and sent them to me for autographs. All that attention was flattering, but it is actually people like William Rounds with diabetes much longer than me who deserve most of the credit for living long lives with diabetes.

William Rounds was born in 1923 and diagnosed when he was 11 months old. That was the year that insulin was first made available to the general public. He and his parents watched his urine glucose levels closely and he never missed a day of school.

Rounds is now 86 and has been Type 1 for 86 years. It is thought that he may have lived longer with Type 1 diabetes than anyone else in the world. "He's always taken good care of himself" says his wife, Dorothy. "He accepted that it was his problem to deal with and he did." He is now retired and living in Texas. Rounds appears on the front cover of the October, 2008, issue of the *Diabetes Forecast.*

164

William Rounds is my hero. He started dealing with his diabetes 22 years before I was diagnosed. His story gives me hope that I might equal his record. Rounds never knew life any other way. I was diagnosed at 6 years of age but there are only brief glimpses of my life before that time, so it is easy for me to identify with William Rounds in many ways.

There were eleven long living diabetics in that magazine. Most of them have been diabetics longer than me. The links for William Rounds, myself, and the other diabetics in that issue appear below.

My picture as it appears in the magazine.

****

References for Chapter 21.

Milewski, Mary. *Diabetes Health*. "Brothers' Diabetes Spans History of Insulin". December, 2008.

Colberg, Sheri R. & Edelman, Steven V. *Diabetes Health.*
After All These Years: 83 Years of Living Well With
Diabetes". May, 2007.

Curry, Andrew. *Diabetes Forecast.* "Long Lives, Lived
Well". October, 2008.

Neithercott, Tracey. *Diabetes Forecast.* "Long Live Living
Long". October, 2008.

CHAPTER 22....Why Do Some Type 1's Live Long Lives Without Complications?

During the first 40 years of my diabetic life I had no real knowledge of how to properly manage my diabetes. It is obvious that I was running very high blood glucose levels back then, but did not know how dangerous that was. Potential complications that could result from high blood glucose levels were revealed to me in the late 1970's. Dr. B. was in charge of the kidney patients on dialysis at the Kingston Hospital at that time. Many of them were diabetics. He told me of other complications that could occur with diabetics who had poor control for a prolonged period of time.

Dr. D. in Roanoke had told me my diabetes was different when we discussed my doing so well. His statement gave me confidence. Dr. B's. discussion did not frighten me. I felt that my strict diabetes management and the success that I had for 40 years would enable me to avoid bad complications. That was just wishful thinking, but my wish has come true. Now, in the year 2009, I am 70 and have had Type 1 diabetes for 64 years, without any serious complications.

In April, 2009, I started a discussion on several diabetes sites with the title "Why Do Some Type 1s Live Long Lives Without Complications". One reply on diabetesforums.com caught my eye. A member of that site found an article that suggested that the beef and pork insulins that so many of us older diabetics used contained C-peptide. Perhaps that C-peptide helped protect us from diabetes related complications.

C-peptide does nothing to lower blood sugar, but recent

research is finding that it might have a role in preventing diabetes complications. Since the insulin taken from pigs and cows worked for us early diabetics and C-peptide has been found in those insulins, it seems reasonable that the C-peptide would have worked for us as well. The C-peptide may have helped me to avoid complications for all those years while using the beef and pork insulins.

C-peptide is a byproduct of insulin production. The level of C-peptide is a gauge of how much insulin is being produced in the body. C-peptide functions in repair of the muscular layer of the arteries and is also helpful in treating many complications experienced by Type 1 diabetics. It is used in treating diabetic neuropathy, it prevents diabetic nephropathy in the kidneys, and improves blood flow in the heart for diabetic patients.

In healthy individuals pancreatic beta-cells produce proinsulin. Proinsulin splits into C-peptide and insulin, both of which are released into circulation.

In Type 1 diabetes patients pancreatic beta-cells cease to function, no proinsulin is produced, and neither insulin nor C-peptide are formed. Long-term complications of diabetes frequently develop despite insulin therapy and good blood glucose control.

C-peptide is obviously useful to Type 1 diabetics, but it is not present in modern day insulins. Some patients suffered allergic reactions to the C-peptide in beef and pork insulins used in the past. That was, however, when the methods for purification for those insulins were less advanced. While researching this topic I have found no other reason for C-peptide not being included in the insulins we are currently using.

In 1997 research was done by Eli Lilly, the company that

produces so much of the insulin used today. Their studies involved rodents and not humans, but it was shown that C-Peptide might prevent and even reverse cardiovascular disease and nerve damage in diabetic patients. Despite these findings the company never pursued developing a product containing C-peptide. In 2007 a representative of the company did indicate that they were pursuing development of drugs to treat diabetes complications. I wonder if those drugs will contain C-peptide.

****

In the February, 2009, issue of *Diabetes Care* there is a report involving a study of 471 Type 1 diabetics. The subjects were born during the 1945-2004 time period and they had been examined one or more times during the years 1994-2004. Beta cell secretion was observed in some of the people who had been diabetic for a long time. It was found that there were fewer instances of microvascular complications among the Type 1 diabetics who had higher fasting C-peptide values. There were 41% fewer instances of microvascular complications among patients whose C-peptide values were at least 0.06. It should be noted that this pattern was not observed with macrovascular complications.

NOTE: Microvascular complications pertain to the smaller blood vessels and include retinopathy, neuropathy and kidney failure.
Macrovascular diabetes complications include heart disease, stroke, and diseases in the larger arteries of the limbs.

****

The Joslin Diabetes Center in Boston is currently studying long term Type 1 diabetics who have lived with their diabetes for 50 years or more. An attempt is being made to determine factors which have allowed these survivors to be resistant to the often seen complications of diabetes. The participants in this study are Joslin Medalists and are all residents of the United States. The Medalist population provides a unique opportunity to study individuals with extreme duration of diabetes. The Joslin Medalist Program and the Medalist Study will be explored further in the next two chapters.

****

"Creative Peptides" is a biopharmaceutical company founded in 1996 and located in Stockholm, Sweden. Their purpose is to develop drugs which will help treat long-term complications of Type 1 diabetes.

Since modern day insulins do not contain C-peptide, Creative Peptides has developed a product for C-peptide replacement in Type 1 diabetics. The purpose of C-peptide replacement is to improve sensory nerve dysfunction and structural abnormalities, to improve autonomic nerve function (heart rate variability), to improve renal dysfunction and to increase regional blood flow.

Clinical studies involving the use of this product in more than 400 Type 1 diabetics have shown encouraging results with patients having nerve and kidney damage. There were no C-peptide related adverse reactions seen while treating these patients. Positive results have also been seen in a group of more than 160 Type 1 diabetics with peripheral neuropathy.

The Swedish company has filed a patent on the product used for C-peptide replacement. I hope they are successful with this and other drugs and that Type 1 diabetics can receive C-peptide with great results.

****

There is a Type 1 diabetic who writes very informative messages on dlife.com. I will refer to him as Mr. Z. He has done much research in books, journals and such, and has found things I have not heard or seen online. All my research has been done online and so it is refreshing to hear these findings from alternate sources. Mr. Z has always impressed me with his replies to many of us on that site. He has given me permission to quote him on his posts on the website. One of Mr. Z's posts appears below.

"The main theory now proposed to explain why some people live 50 years and more with type 1 diabetes and never get complications no matter what their degree or blood sugar control, while others are dead from complications within 20 years of onset despite excellent control, is that people have different levels of the enzymes required to metabolize excess blood glucose, which is not the harmful element, to advanced glycation end products, which are what do the damage. So because some people lack the enzymes necessary to complete the chain from high blood sugar to damaging advanced glycation endproducts, their blood sugar levels really don't matter. In contrast, those with a heavy dose of the necessary enzymes can suffer complications even at a near normal glucose level.

An example of the latter type of patient, the converse of those who have type 1 diabetes for many years without complications, was reported in 'Kidney International' in 1986. He had all the classic type 1 diabetic complications in severe degree, but he wasn't diabetic! He had never had high blood sugar, and a glucose tolerance test showed a normal result. The only explanation was that his enzyme complement was such that he could even form an enormous load of toxic glycation end products from a perfectly normal blood sugar level."

At another time Mr. Z told us more about the previous topic. Here is his follow-up.

"The passage relates to the 'Steno Hypothesis,' named after the diabetes center in Denmark where it was first developed. The hypothesis argues that genetic variations among type 1 diabetics determine the nature and amount of their available enzymes for metabolizing heparin sulphate, and this in turn determines their susceptibility to the negative effects of excess glucose. In those patients who lack the necessary enzymes to metabolize excess glucose to its toxic form in advanced glycation end products, the complications simply cannot develop. This also explains the action of Benfotiamine in preventing excess glucose from causing complications, since Benfotiamine blocks the enzymatic action necessary to transform surplus glucose into toxic advanced glycation endproducts. So if you are not genetically lucky in the enzymes you inherited, then you can compensate for this by taking Benfotiamine. See T. Deckert, et al, "Genetic Variation in Enzyme Character Determines Susceptibility to Glucose" Diabetologia, vol. 32, no. 4, p. 219 (1989)."

If I could write like Mr. Z, I would write more books. I find his posts very interesting.

****

On April7, 2009, I joined an online chat with Gary Scheiner on diabetestalkfest.com. Gary is a well known author of several wonderful books on diabetes and self management, including *Think Like A Pancreas* During that chat I asked Gary if he knew any people who have had diabetes for more than 60 years, without any complications.

This was a moderated chat and the questions being asked were sent to Gary in the order they were asked. The chat was scheduled for one hour and the time had expired, but Gary took the time to answer my question. Here is his reply: "Richard - In fact, I do. A 68-year diabetic woman. Research is showing that there is a genetic sequence that protects some people against microvascular and neural complications." That response meant very much to me. The following week I joined a second chat with Gary on his own website, and he gave me permission to use his statement in my book.

I have seen many Type 1 diabetics write about their doctors telling them that living for 20 years without complications usually indicates that they will not develop complications as long as they maintain good control. The fact that many doctors are telling their patients that suggests there is some basis for the statement. The following is one of the many replies that mention the "20 year" statement.

On May 9, 2009, a Type 1 diabetic made a reply to the discussion "Why Do Some Type 1's Live Long Lives Without Complications?". Here is his statement:

"Richard, it gives me a good feeling that you are doing so well - that is really encouraging. My doc told me about this genetical predisposition too. If a T1 lives for more that 20 years with this disease and has not developed complications then it is quite likely that he has some of the protective genes. Being beyond these 20 years without complications is comforting for me. But at the same time it is scary. Because it also means that some of us will not have the chance to achieve that - even with quite good numbers - since their genes can not cope that well with BG fluctuations. It seems that we all need this extra portion of luck. So let us hope for the best and try as hard as we can."

This gentleman's words make a lot of sense to me. We Type 1's who have lived a very long time with diabetes have indeed hoped for the best and we have tried as hard as we could. None of us know for certain why we have been so fortunate. We have managed to avoid serious complications in order to live so long with our diabetes. Our long lives without complications is our reward.

****

The National Institute of Diabetes and Digestive and Kidney Diseases
funded a study of Type 1 diabetics from 1983 to 1993. The study became known as the Diabetes Control and Complications Trial (DCCT). There were 1,441 Type 1 diabetics who volunteered for the study. These volunteers of ages 13 to 39 came from 29 medical centers in the United States and Canada.

All the volunteers were required to have had diabetes for at least 1 year, but no longer than 15 years. They were also required to have no more than early signs of diabetic eye disease.

The volunteers were randomly assigned to each of two treatment groups. In one group standard blood glucose control was applied. The members of the other group used intensive control, which required keeping their A1c's as close as possible to 6 percent, or less. diabetes complications involving the eyes, kidneys and other nerve damage in the two groups were then compared.

The diabetes complications under study were shown to occur and progress at a much slower pace among the individuals using intensive control. This kind of control also helped the subjects who had a previous history of poor control.

The DCCT findings showed that intensive blood glucose control reduced the risk of eye disease by 76%, kidney disease by 50% and nerve disease by 60%.

After the DCCT ended there was a follow-up study of more than 90% of the volunteers. This study was called the Epidemiology of Diabetes Interventions and Complications (EDIC). Heart attack, stroke, needed heart surgery, as well as complications involving the eye, kidney, and nerves were assessed. Intensive control versus standard control was still under study by the EDIC. The quality of life while using intensive control as well as its cost-effectiveness were studied.

The EDIC study showed that intensive blood glucose control reduced the risk of any cardiovascular disease event by 42% and fatal heart attack, stroke, or death from cardiovascular causes by 57%.

The EDIC has continued these studies over the intervening years. In the July 27, 2009 issue of the Archives of internal Medicine the EDIC revealed that "...microvascular and cardiovascular complications of type 1 diabetes are cut in half for patients with near-normal glucose".

The most important factors in preventing diabetes complications are considered to be the control of blood glucose, blood pressure and blood lipid levels. Both Type 1 and Type 2 diabetics will benefit from this kind of control.

CHAPTER 23....The Joslin Medalist Program and Study

The Joslin Medalist Program

The Joslin Diabetes Center in Boston, Massachusetts, gives medals to diabetics who have been insulin dependent for for 50 and 75 years.

Here is a copy of the letter I received from Joslin after inquiring about getting a medal. The envelope contained an application form.

"Thank you very much for your interest in Joslin Diabetes Center's Medal Program. Enclosed please find all of the information you will need to apply for a 25-Year Certificate or our 50- and 75-Year Medals, including a single application that can be used for all three awards.

Below are some facts about Joslin Diabetes Center's Medal Program. The awards are presented on an ongoing basis to people with diabetes who have been insulin-dependent continuously for at least 25 years.

Since the program began in 1970, Joslin has awarded approximately 2,400 50-Year Medals.
Also since this time, more than 550 certificates have been awarded to people who have been insulin-dependent for 25 to 49 years.
Joslin Diabetes Center has awarded medals to recipients throughout the world—including individuals from Australia, Brazil, Canada, England, Hungary, Japan, the Netherlands, Pakistan, the Philippines, Russia, South America, Spain, Sweden and Switzerland.
From 1996-2005, Joslin has also awarded 17 distinctive 75-Year medals to 10 men and six women who lived in Mass., R.I., Fla., Conn., Wash., Pa., Ga., Wis., Va., Ind., N.Y.,

Ohio, Md., and one international award to a woman in New Zealand."

For more information about the program, you can u contact:

Medalist Program Coordinator
Joslin Diabetes Center, Suite 745
One Joslin Place
Boston, MA 02215
Phone: (617) 732-2412
Fax: (617) 732-2692
E-mail: medals@joslin.harvard.edu

How To Obtain A Joslin Medal.

There are links below containing information about the Joslin Medalist Program. If you scroll to the bottom of the page on the first link, you will find a printable application form. They want proof that you have been a diabetic for at least 50 years. When I saw that form a few years ago, becoming a Medalist seemed impossible. My parents were deceased, my doctor from my diagnosis year was deceased, and the hospital where I was admitted keeps records for only the past 10 years. There was no proof I had diabetes for at least 50 years.

Then a lady emailed me and explained how she had no proof, but still became a Medalist. Two of her friends who knew her at the time she was diagnosed wrote letters and told what they remembered about her diabetes. Those letters resulted in her getting her medal.

I asked my sister and cousin to write letters telling about their memories of what happened in those early years after I was diagnosed . They sent their letters to me and I sent them along with my application form to the Joslin Diabetes

Center in Boston, MA. They were accepted as proof and my medal arrived in August, 2009.

If you want the medal, you have had diabetes for at least 50 years, and you have proof, then it is easy to apply. If you do not have proof, you can have people who knew you during the year you were diagnosed, or the next few years after the diagnosis write letters for you. Two or three letters are requested if there is no other proof you can give them.

Here are my certificate and medal, received in August, 2009.

The 50 year certificate.

CERTIFICATE OF ACHIEVEMENT

Presented to

Richard A. Vaughn

for living courageously
with diabetes for
50 years

J Joslin Diabetes Center

August 24, 2009

Date

Ranch C. Kimball

On the front of the Joslin medal

On the back.

I had the 64'th anniversary of my diagnosis on Sept. 15, 2009, so I will hopefully receive my 75 year medal in 2020.

****

The Joslin Medalist Study

The Joslin Medalist Study began in April 2005 to identify physiological, clinical, genetic and other factors shared by the Medalists. All Medalists have had Type 1 diabetes for 50 years or more.

On June 12, 2006, the American Diabetes Association 66th Annual Scientific Sessions were held. It was reported that some of the Joslin Medalists still had C-peptide secretion. These individuals had been Type 1 for 50 years or more and some of them tested positive for antibodies to islet cells which showed that some islet function was still present. 48% of the group had very little or no microvascular complications. This shows that long term diabetics do not always experience these complications.

"It is surprising that some Medalists still have c-peptide secretion, a sign of insulin production, and some are positive for antibodies to the islets, another sign that some islet function or mass still is present. The significance of these findings is that even after such a prolonged period of diabetes, some patients still have residual islet function," said George L. King, M.D., the study's lead author. Dr. King is Joslin's Research Director, Head of the Section on Vascular Cell Biology, head of Joslin's 50-Year Medalist Study and a Professor of Medicine at Harvard Medical School.

The study that was presented at the ADA meeting involved 326 patients with more than 50 years of insulin-dependent diabetes. In a subset of 125 of these people with Type 1 diabetes, 12.7 percent had a C-peptide level greater than 0.3 mg/ml, which indicates that they have active islet cells and some insulin production.

Researchers and doctors involved with the study feel that kidney or eye disease might be prevented if the reason for the lack of complications could be found. Lifestyle and longevity genes are also being considered as possible contributors to the development of complications.

"The findings are phenomenal," said Hillary Keenan, Ph.D., research associate at Joslin, and co-investigator on the 50-Year Medalist Study, who will present the findings. "This is the first study to look at the specific biomarkers for islet cell presence in people with a 50-year duration of insulin-dependent diabetes."

The study opens new avenues for research and treatment of Type 1 diabetes. "If a way can be found to stimulate islet growth, we could improve their diabetes and reduce insulin usage or better control blood glucose levels. If islets were returned to normal levels, they wouldn't need to take insulin," said Dr. King. This is an ongoing study. Thus far the data show that Type 1 diabetics who have lived with their diabetes for 50 years or more are much less likely to experience nephropathy and retinopathy.

When I applied for my medal an application form was sent to me. A Joslin Medalist Study update, dated Fall 2008, was included in that mailing. At that time, 400 Medalists had participated in the Study. The goal was to include 350 more participants by April, 2011.

In June, 2008, it was revealed that 17% of the Medalist participants were still producing some insulin. Other statements concerning the participants, at that time, are as follows: average age at diagnosis was 11 years old; average duration of diabetes was 57 years; average insulin dose per day was 0.5 units per kilogram or 2.2 pounds. The average age of the Medalists examined, as of December 2007, was 68 years, with no differences in gender.

Studies in new areas are now under way. These studies include "genetics, the presence of autoantibodies and blood markers of diabetic complications". The whole human genes is being scanned in order "to examine the associations of different characteristics with all of a person's genetic material". The relationship between retinopathy and C-peptide production is being studied. The

184

proteins that result from the genetic findings "...will also be studied to determine if the gene errors translate to differences in protein expression...". It is hoped that these findings will lead to "potential targets for developing treatments".

Funding for the study is being provided by the Juvenile Diabetes Research Foundation (JDRF).

Below is a link to the Joslin Medalist Study.

http://www.joslin.org/1083_3480.asp

CHAPTER 24.... My Participation In The Joslin Medalist Study

When I received my Joslin medal in the mail there was an application form enclosed for participation in the Medalist Study. I sent my application to the Joslin Diabetes Center, and in mid September a lady named Leah called to tell me that I was accepted as a participant in the study. She said my transportation and lodging expenses would be paid by the program. There would be a blood work-up and an examination of my eyes, kidneys and nervous system. This was very exciting! I was so anxious to find if there were functioning beta cells and C-peptide in my pancreas. Anita was scheduled for a complete knee replacement surgery on Sept. 29 so we scheduled my date for going to Boston on November 30. This would give Anita time for completing post-op physical therapy, so she could be more comfortable during our visit in Boston.

There were approximately 20 pages on the forms I filled out as part of my preparation for the study. Personal history, information about my family and relatives, my daily food schedule, exercise schedule, and many other items were explored.

As part of my preparation I was supposed to have a listing of all my A1c's that had ever been done. My doctor was very cooperative, but there were several gaps in the list. The years 1990-1994 were not available. There are many other gaps as well. I hoped this incomplete list would be acceptable at Joslin on Nov 30.

Below are the A1c's that my doctor was able to retrieve from his files:

1980...10.6, 9.6, 9.0
1981...11.8
1983...9.2
1984...9.2, 9.7, 8.9
1986...11.1
1987...8.0, 9.8, 10.3
1988...10.5, 7.7, 7.7
1989...7.3
1995...6.8
1997...6.0, 5.4
1998...6.5
1999...6.8, 6.7, 6.5
2000...6.3, 6.1, 5.5
2001...5.8, 6.0, 5.6, 6.0
2002...6.0, 6.4, 6.2, 6.0
2003...5.6, 5.4, 5.9
2004...5.9, 5.7, 5.8, 5.6
2005...5.6, 5.8
2006...5.6, 5.7
2007...5.5, 5.6, 5.7, 6.1
2008...5.7, 5.9, 5.7, 5.6
2009...5.6, 5.8, 5.8

Notice the drop from the 10's to the 7's in early 1988. That is when I finally found that diabetics should follow a low carb diet.

I took only one injection of beef and pork insulin per day during my first 40+ years. Can you imagine what my A1c's would have been during those years? Those were the years before my doctor started having my A1c's done.

I feel so lucky to be alive and healthy, without complications. Is it good genes? It is very doubtful that C-peptide is protecting me. I asked Dr. B. to include a C-peptide test in my September blood testing. The report showed that my C-peptide is less than 0.1. That suggests that I produce almost no insulin. There has to be some other factor(s) that have protected me all these years. I hoped that the Joslin Study would help answer that question.

On Sunday, November 29, we drove to Boston. It was the Sunday after Thanksgiving and we were concerned about very heavy traffic, but I had purchased a GPS that made the trip very easy. We stayed at the Holiday Inn in the Brookline section of Boston. It was a wonderful hotel, the staff members there were very helpful and friendly.

Two of my friends from the diabetesdaily.com website live in the Boston area. We met them and the four of us had dinner that evening. Part of my preparation for the Medalist Study was to double my usual carb intake at dinner, on both Saturday and Sunday. I ate pasta and estimated the carbs at 70g. My estimation must have been totally wrong since my blood sugar was 184 in the late evening. Dr. King had called me at home and requested that I have very tight control for the week before our visit. I was disappointed in the high test result, but my blood sugar was very good the the next morning.

A shuttle provided by the hotel took us to The Joslin Center at 7 AM, Monday morning. We were met by Leah, the same young lady who had phoned me about being accepted as a participant that day. She took us to a room on the third floor. Anita sat in a comfortable chair in the room while all the testing was done. Leah explained that Dr. King could not be there that day. Leah and another staff member took charge of my testing. Many test tubes of blood were taken from my arm.

Fasting was required starting at midnight on Sunday and I

was required to skip breakfast on the testing date. An IV and catheter were placed in my arm. After the initial blood samples were taken I was given a tall glass of vanilla flavored glucose. Leah called it a "vanilla milkshake". UGH! If vanilla milkshakes taste like that, I have not been missing anything all these years. The doubling of my carbs for dinner the previous two nights, combined with the glucose drink, was called a "mixed meal tolerance test".

Blood samples were taken every 30 minutes for the next two hours. At the end of the first hour my BG was 244. After two hours, my BG was 320. Since my BG had continued rising for the entire 2 hours it was evident that there was little or no insulin being produced in my body. Leah told us that some Medalists had lower numbers at the two hour mark than after only one hour. That showed they were still producing some insulin, even though they had been diabetic for more than 50 years. I was disappointed, but not surprised, that my body seemed to have no insulin production.

I was permitted to take a dose of insulin at that time. I needed 20 units of Humalog. The glucose drink made me feel lousy and somewhat nauseous. After a brief test on my feet for neuropathy we were taken to the Beetham Eye Institute, Joslin's eye center, in another part of the building. My feeling of nausea made it difficult for me to concentrate when the staff members at the eye center asked me questions.

I was concerned that my high blood sugar would have some effect on my eyes during the exam. Two staff members explained that it would not affect my eyes since cataracts had been removed from both of my eyes. The artificial lenses implanted in my eyes would not be affected during my exam. Diabetics who still had their own eye lenses, the ones they had since birth, could experience swelling and wrinkling in their retinas and lenses if they had high blood sugar during an eye exam. That swelling causes blurred vision, and would definitely have an effect on eye exams.

Dr. Shah is a brilliant opthamologist and she gave me the most thorough eye exam I have ever had. Pictures were taken of the backs of my eyeballs. I had never had that done by any other doctor. There were a couple of minor abnormalities, but I was told that my eyes were in very good shape. Dr. Shah said that copies of my pictures and report would be sent to my home in two weeks time. My opthamologist in Kingston will be interested in seeing them.

I finally had a much better BG level by 5 PM and we ate dinner at the hotel. That was my first food for that day. I had gone 22 hours without eating any food. We had anticipated that the testing would make me feel out of sorts and I would not be able to drive home that afternoon. We had reserved our room for Monday night. We drove home Tuesday morning.

While driving home I started thinking that the eye exam should be done before the glucose tolerance test. That would have permitted me to feel normal and alert during the exam. Diabetics who could be affected by high blood sugar during the exam would have a more normal blood sugar level while in the eye center, if the glucose tolerance test had not been done beforehand.

A few days after we got home we were notified by Liberty, the company that sends me my diabetes supplies, that I had been approved for using a CGMS (continuous glucose monitoring system). It is very expensive to use a CGMS and I was very happy that my insurance had agreed to pay my expenses. My pump has improved my control very much, but I had hoped a CGMS would help me prevent the highs and lows that I still experience.

Approximately one week after we were home we received my lab reports from Joslin. The results were very good and they showed that I had good health. The only numbers that concerned me were a few from my Complete Blood Count which showed some mild abnormalities: WBC (White blood cell)-4.3, RBC (Red blood cell)-3.78, HGB-12.8, HCT-38, PLT-126..... all those are somewhat low. Then there was: MCV-100.6, MCH-33.8...both of those are somewhat high. This happens every time I have anemia. The anemia started after radiation treatment for my prostate cancer in 2003. I take vitamin B12 and some iron tablets whenever I have anemia. After several months my anemia is gone, my blood count is normal and there is no more problem. My anemia has been occurring once per year, but it is easy to control with the vitamin supplements.

My lab report showed: Cholesterol-126, HDL-60, LDL-52, Trig-69, A1c-5.8. My BP was 126 over 64. The rest of the report also showed good numbers, much the same as my September report done in Kingston.

Dr. King is usually available to meet the Medalists when they are at Joslin for participation in the Study, but he was not available the day we were there. There were questions I had wanted to ask Dr. King. Leah told me I could email the questions to her and Dr. King would reply. I sent an email containing three questions. Dr. King was very gracious and sent me answers to those questions.

You will find my questions and Dr. King's answers in the following paragraphs.

Question #1....I have no relatives with Type 1. I feel that my diabetes was caused by childhood diseases (mumps and chicken pox) when I was 5. Immediately after that period of time I began displaying the classic symptoms of Type 1. There was a question posed on a diabetes website : "What Caused Your Type 1?". Most responses listed causes other than a genetic link. Almost all of those individuals who felt that their Type 1 was caused by diseases seemed to have no serious complications. Is it possible that when Type 1 is caused by disease then there is less likelihood of developing complications?

Dr. King's reply..."The question of the causes of type 1 diabetes is clearly very important. It is very common to have childhood diseases associated with the onset of diabetes. However, it is unclear whether these childhood diseases are causing type 1 DM. It is clear that if you don't have the genes which makes you at risk for diabetes, then it is very unlikely that you will develop diabetes. The risk of complications for the eyes, kidney and nervous system is mainly related to glucose control for the non-Medalist diabetic patients. Thus, the type of diabetes is not so critical but the glucose control after getting diabetes is very important."

Question #2....I have often thought that the presence of C-peptide in long term Type 1 diabetics might explain their longevity and lack of complications. There have been studies that seemed to imply that. I thought that I might have a C-peptide level much like the Study participants whose C-peptides were 0.3 or greater. I asked my doctor to include a C-peptide test in my September lab work. It showed that my C-peptide is less than 0.1. I was disappointed. Your assistant said that there are other participants like me who have a very low C-peptide, but do not have complications. I suppose that there must be some avenue(s), in addition to a low C-peptide, that may explain our lack of complications after 50 years or more.

Dr. King's reply...."In general, type 1 diabetic patients with residual insulin production have better glucose control and thus fewer complications. However, this relationship does not seem to apply to the Medalists."[/b]

Question #3...."Creative Peptides" is a biopharmaceutical company founded in 1996 and located in Stockholm, Sweden. Their purpose is to develop drugs which will help treat long-term complications of Type 1 diabetes. Creative Peptides has developed a product for C-peptide replacement in Type 1 diabetics. Clinical studies involving the use of this product in more than 400 Type 1 diabetics have shown encouraging results with patients having nerve and kidney damage. There were no C-peptide related adverse reactions seen while treating these patients. Positive results have also been seen in a group of more than 160 Type 1 diabetics with peripheral neuropathy. The Swedish company has filed a patent on the product used for C-peptide replacement. I hope they are successful with this and other drugs and that Type 1 diabetics can receive C-peptide with great results.

Dr. King's reply...."C-peptide for treatments of diabetic complications. There are some preliminary data to suggest C-peptide may help but it is very unclear. Type 2 diabetic patients have elevated levels of c-peptide yet they have many of the same complications as type 1 diabetic patients. If c-peptide is helpful, I believe the effect will be very small."

The Medalists have been Type 1 for 50 years or more and most of them have no complications, or no serious complications. It has been clear to me that the Medalists are a separate group unto themselves in that so many of them have no complications even though they have little or no insulin production. Many of them have not had a history of good diabetes care. I ran very high blood sugar for most of

194

my life, until modern times, but I do not have complications. I gather that most of the Medalists have a similar history. There was no guide to good diabetes control during most of their lifetimes. It seems clear to me that there has to be some explanation for their success stories. The Joslin Medalist Study is ongoing and there may be very important findings when it concludes in 2011.

Our trip to Boston and the Joslin Diabetes Center was very important to me. I hope so very much that the results of the Joslin Diabetes Study will reveal some reasons why we Medalists have lived so long without serious complications caused by our diabetes. Those reasons, if found, might lead to a treatment for younger and more recently diagnosed Type 1's so they can avoid diabetes related complications and have healthier lives.

AFTERWORD

In my earlier years I was not very good about looking for information about diabetes. My doctors were my guides. Of course there was very little knowledge about diabetes in the 1940's, when I was diagnosed. This was still true in the 1950's, and to a large degree, in the 1960's. I coasted along and did no research of any kind. There may have been books about diabetes back then, but it never occurred to me look for them. If books had been available in the early years, maybe low carb dieting would have been mentioned. That could have given me much better control, and I might have avoided so many years of terribly high blood sugar that led to my several mild complications that developed in later years.

Putting things off has always been a bad habit of mine. In the 1980s Dr. B. recommended that I use an insulin pump and that I should visit the Joslin Diabetes Center for a thorough examination. I chose not to follow his advice. My body was so accustomed to running high blood sugar and everything seemed great. Insulin pumps were being used for more than 20 years before I started pumping in 2007. I was running a lot of highs and lows back then and a pump would really have helped me. My stubbornness and refusing to take advantage of new technology could have been dangerous to my health.

When computers and the internet became available diabetes support groups and online research entered the picture. The internet was up and running many years before I joined my first support group in 2006. So that was another delay on my part. Why did I put off making these changes that would have greatly improved my life and my health? Stubbornness and contentment with my life as it was did not enable me to realize how much better it could be.

I hope that those of you who read my story do not make these mistakes. If you are having reasonably good control of your diabetes, don't assume that you should ignore newly developed technology, new medicines, pumps, a CGMS and the like. Research these things, ask your doctor(s) about them, and ask the experienced diabetics online about them. Let the experienced diabetics online share their experience with you. Take advantage of new developments and don't put things off that can give you better contro. Taking advantage of available sources may give a better and longer life, without serious complications that might otherwise occur.

My glucose meter, pump, and my new Dexcom CGMS are responsible for my having the best control ever. I never dreamed that control this good would ever be possible. I had minor complications with my diabetes, but they were temporary. Now I am enjoying my retirement and my diabetes is complication-free.

As discussed in the preceding chapter research has suggested that my having had Type 1 diabetes for 64 years and being so healthy may be due to my having a "genetic sequence" that protects me from diabetes complications. My doctors have stated that they have no idea why I have been so fortunate. I have my own theory. In my first chapter it was mentioned that I had chickenpox and mumps within a few months time in 1945, and the symptoms of my diabetes appeared shortly after those illnesses. Despite statements made by some experts I am still convinced that those diseases attacked my five year old body, damaged my pancreas, and caused my diabetes.

There have been no relatives on my family tree with Type 1 diabetes. My diabetes apparently developed in some way other than through the genes from a relative. Therefore, my diabetes may be less likely to be associated with the complications that so many diabetics experience. This is just my own theory and I have no foundation for it. It is my gut feeling and nothing more. During my very early years my doctor said I had "something like diabetes", but not like conventional diabetes. That may be true. My Type 1 diabetes has been very different, in many ways, from the Type 1 diabetes that I have read and heard about from so many other diabetics.

I am blessed to have had a very wonderful and, in my opinion, very healthy life for 70 years. I am thankful for my wonderful family and I am very, very thankful that no other member of my family has diabetes.

The lines on my face clearly show my age,
So take heed and listen to this old sage,
Don't spend your life like a bird in a cage,
Take charge of your lives, that's the rage!

I hope you have learned from this old critter,
I ain't no prize but I never was a quitter!
Diabetic all these years but I'm not bitter,
I love my life and my wife and I couldn't be fitter!!

****

I had insulin injections for 61 years. I started pumping insulin on 6/19/07. I have told friends that I intend to pump insulin for 61 years. Since I was 6 when diagnosed that will make me 6 + 61 + 61 = 128 years old on Sept. 10, 2067. I plan to have a whale of a birthday party on that date. All of my readers are all invited!!! Now, who is going to host the party???

Blogs

The Smell Of Alcohol

When I was diagnosed in 1945 there were no diabetes types, all of us were given insulin to help with our fight against high blood sugar. My family lived in a small four room house that was not insulated. There was no insulation in the attic, or in the walls, so we stayed very cold in the winter time. It was very cold in the morning when I had to take my insulin. My father loaded the big glass syringe with my insulin, and brought a big wad of cotton he had dipped in rubbing alcohol. I lowered my pants and felt the cold air in the room. It made me shiver as I rubbed a spot on top of my upper leg. The alcohol would run down my leg, and it felt icy cold when it did that. I hated everything about taking those shots. Even the smell of that alcohol was very unpleasant. The needles were very long and thick and my father pushed it into the muscle on top of my cold, shivering leg. I hated the cold, the pain and the smell of the alcohol.

Fast forward to the year 1963. I was visiting my girlfriend, Anita, at her home, and meeting her parents for the first time. The meal served that evening was very good, but there was an unpleasant odor of alcohol in my glass. I had never tasted alcohol, my parents never had alcoholic beverages in our home. It was white wine in my glass, and I wished it was water. I hated the taste and the smell of the wine. After explaining that I did not drink alcohol, Anita's mother took my wine and brought me water. I hesitated doing that, I did not want to upset that evening in any way. The rest of the evening went very smoothly. Later that evening, I proposed to Anita in the downstairs family room in front of a warm fire her father had built in the fireplace. She said YES and we were very happy!!!

I did not taste alcohol again until 1972, while visiting the home of the president of the college, where I was teaching. He brought me a glass with with some vodka in it. There it was again, the awful smell of alcohol. I pretended to sip some of the drink. When my host was greeting some other guests, I poured the vodka on the ground and asked for some sparkling water. I have never tasted of alcohol since that day.

It was not until last year that it dawned on me that my hatred of the smell of alcoholic beverages stems back to the time I was taking those shots during my childhood. I learned to hate the smell of alcohol then, and I hate it just as much now. I don't mind being with people who drink as long as they are not drunk, but I hate the smell of their drinks. It can actually take my appetite away.

My not drinking is undoubtedly due to my hating the smell of alcohol. That is probably a good thing. Maybe I should be grateful for the shots during my early years of diabetes. Who would have thought that experience would lead to my never drinking?

Anita and my younger son do not drink, but my older son does have some wine with his dinner.

****

My Lifetime Experience With Weight Control

When diagnosed in 1945 I had lost weight and remained very skinny for several years. When fully grown I had a very normal weight. With a height of 6 feet, 2 inches and a large frame, my ideal weight was 185 pounds. My meals and snacks were very high in carbs until 1988 when I found that a low carb diet is best for diabetics. It was typical for me to eat hundreds of carbs every day. The only restriction that my doctors had made was that I should avoid sugar. It seemed that all foods were OK as long as they did not contain sugar. My weight stayed within 5 pounds of my ideal weight from my late teen years until the 1990's. You can see me in the early chapters of this book. There was no overweight present there.

It was in the 1990's that I stopped using beef/pork insulins and started using modern day insulins. That caused me to gain a lot of weight. You can see me at my heaviest weight below.

After reducing my carb intake to 130g per day and exercising every day, I have lost 34 pounds and need to lose only 23 more pounds. That took several years to accomplish. My pictures in the later chapters in 2008 and 2009 show me after my weight loss. Very careful dieting and exercise will enable me to lose more weight. It is very unhealthy for a diabetic to be very much overweight.

****

My grand daughter is growing up much too fast!!!

Vanessa, age 6, 2009

Jason, age 2, 2009

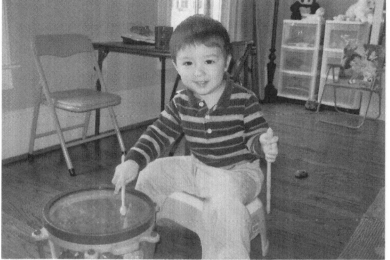

Recommended Websites and Books

I visited my first online diabetes website on July 4, 2006. There was so much information about diabetes there, things I had never known before. The support group was so helpful, and I pitched in and truly enjoyed the participation. My long life with diabetes gave me the experiences that I shared with my fellow diabetics. I am now a member of many diabetes sites, and one of my favorite pastimes is to post information and help my fellow diabetics in the support groups on those sites. The diabetes websites I have joined are listed below.

Websites

diabetesdaily.com - A rapidly growing site with very friendly members who will readily answer your questions and offer you great support. The site is frequently updated and is computer friendly. A very good chat room can be found there. This site is well moferated. I have many good friends on this site, and spend a lot of time there.

tudiabetes.com - Another very friendly support group can be found here. I have found many interesting discussions on this site. I especially like the many common interest groups here. The Seniors group, and the Dexcom Users group are two of the groups I enjoy.

diabetesforums.com - A large site with many members who will respond to your questions, and give you much support. There have been so many great discussions on this site.

childrenwithdiabetes.com - This site is a must for parents of diabetic children. It is a wonderful site. It has other forums for diabetics of all types and ages.

dLife.com - A very large website with a vast storehouse of

information, videos and history of diabetes. There is a very large support group on dLife. The dLife TV show on CNBC, every Sunday evening, is wonderful.

dearjanis.com - Janis Roszler's site. It is a small site where my friends and I help each other with our diabetes problems. We also have a lot of fun there. Janis is a CDE, an RD and has written three books on diabetes. She joins in on the help and the fun.

diabeticconnect.com - You will find a very friendly group there. Some discussions will have dozens of replies. I enjoy the many great videos on this site.

diabetesforum.com - A small site that is showing a lot of promise. It is very well designed. I like the format very much. I am a moderator on this site.

diabetes-support.org.uk/joomla - A fine website located in the UK. I really enjoy this site. The peeps there are very knowledgeable and supportive. There is a good chat room there.

diabetesliving.com - A small site with interesting forums. It is very friendly, and has a good chat room.

diabetestalkfest.ning.com - This website has one of the best chat rooms I have seen. It is very popular for that reason.

diabetesteentalk.com - A diabetes site for teens. It has a chat room where diabetic teens can talk to other diabetics of their own age. This site is affiliated with dLife.com.

diabetes.org - The website of the American Diabetes Association. There is a support group there.

Other sites

calorieking.com - This site along with their terrific booklet will enable you to find the number of carbs and calories in almost everything you eat. It is very valuable to diabetics who are following a low carb diet.

joslin.org - The website for the joslin Diabetes Center in Boston

webmd.com - A very reliable source of medical information

Books

Colberg, Sheri R, PhD, Steven V. Edelman, MD. *50 Secrets of the Longest Living People With Diabetes*. New York: Marlowe & Company, 2007.

Hanas, Ragnar, MD, PhD. *Type 1 Diabetes: A Guide For Children, Adolescents, Young Adults-- and Their Caregivers*, 3rd ed. Cambridge, MA: Da Capro Press, 2005.

Hirsch, James. *Cheating Destiny*. Houghton Mifflin, 2006.

Roszler, Janis. *Diabetes On Your Own Terms*. New York: Marlow & Company, 2007.

Roszler, Janis, Donna Rice. *Sex and Diabetes*. Alexandria, VA: American Diabetes Association, 2007.

Rubin, Alan L, MD. *Type 1 Diabetes For Dummies*. Hoboken, NJ: Wiley Publishing, 2010.

Scheiner, Gary. *Think Like A Pancreas: A Practical Guide to Managing Diabetes with Insulin*. Cambridge, MA: Da Capro Press, 2004.

Walsh, John, Ruth Roberts. *Pumping Insulin: Everything You Need for Success on a Smart Insulin Pump*, 4th ed. San Diego, CA: Torrey Pines Press, 2006.

Walsh, John, Ruth Roberts, Timothy Bailey, Chandra Varma. *Using Insulin*. San Diego, CA: Torrey Pines Press, 2003.

Warshaw, Hope, and Karmeen Kulkarni. *Complete Guide to Carb Counting*, 2nd ed. Alexandria, VA: American Diabetes Association, 2004

Made in the USA
Lexington, KY
06 February 2015